Best W...

C.E. ...

Meaning-Centered Leadership

Meaning-Centered Leadership

Skills and Strategies for Increased Employee Well-Being and Organizational Success

Barbara E. Bartels

C. Edward Jackson

ROWMAN & LITTLEFIELD

Lanham • Boulder • New York • London

Published by Rowman & Littlefield
An imprint of The Rowman & Littlefield Publishing Group, Inc.
4501 Forbes Boulevard, Suite 200, Lanham, Maryland 20706
www.rowman.com

6 Tinworth Street, London, SE11 5AL, United Kingdom

British Library Cataloguing in Publication Information Available

Library of Congress Cataloging-in-Publication Data

Names: Bartels, Barbara E., 1964– author. | Jackson, C. Edward, 1961– author.
Title: Meaning-centered leadership : skills and strategies for increased employee
    well-being and organizational success / Barbara E. Bartels, C. Edward Jackson.
Description: Lanham : Rowman & Littlefield, [2021] | Includes bibliographical
    references. | Summary: "This book will inspire readers to create meaning in their
    organizations, increasing employee engagement and fulfillment."—Provided by
    publisher.
Identifiers: LCCN 2020044783 (print) | LCCN 2020044784 (ebook) |
    ISBN 9781475857900 (cloth ; alk. paper) | ISBN 9781475857917
    (paperback ; alk. paper) | ISBN 9781475857924 (epub)
Subjects: LCSH: Leadership. | Employee motivation. | Organizational behavior. |
    Quality of work life.
Classification: LCC HD57.7 .B3678 2021 (print) | LCC HD57.7 (ebook) |
    DDC 658.4/092—dc23
LC record available at https://lccn.loc.gov/2020044783
LC ebook record available at https://lccn.loc.gov/2020044784

♾️ ™ The paper used in this publication meets the minimum requirements of American National Standard for Information Sciences—Permanence of Paper for Printed Library Materials, ANSI/NISO Z39.48-1992.

To my wife, Gail—thank you for bringing meaning into my life since the first time I laid eyes on you. Your ability to see potential where I see doubt has made all the difference.

—C. E. J.

To my children Victoria and Ryan—you complete me! I am so proud of both of you and thankful every day to be your mom. And to my angels in heaven, Tom and Isy Weltzer, thank you for being the best parents ever. I did it, Dad! And, Mom: yes, the "paper" is done! I love you and miss you every day.

—B. E. B.

Contents

Foreword

The workplace is in crisis. I don't have to tell you. You see it every day. Disengaged employees wander the halls like somber zombies, bereft of happiness, let alone ever catching a glimpse of fulfillment. Millions have effectively quit. And stayed.

It's not a new problem. It's old. As are many of the ineffective solutions we throw at the wall in trying to bring the listless back to life. Our efforts to motivate are well-meaning but, well, meaningless, which is ironic, because therein lies the solution.

Meaning.

And that's where the fresh voices of Dr. Ed Jackson and Dr. Barbara Bartels come in. They take what it takes for leaders to make meaning and break it down into bite-size pieces. Their case for grooming *Meaning-Centered Leadership* skills is unassailable and fortified with their 3E model— the inspiring, yet realistic, and pragmatic strategies for meaning-making.

Imagine if you could spur engagement, gift the organization with empowerment, and leverage expertise in an emotionally intelligent way. You now have the tools to do so. You now have the know-how to create trust and continually underscore it with care, concern, and open communication. Your visioning skills will rise to meet the challenge, fueled by enthusiasm and large doses of others-oriented leadership. Wisdom, optimism, and humility will play their role in this call-to-arms as well.

Old problems require a new approach. New approaches reveal treasures. In this case, they come in the form of a reengaged, peak-performing, happy, and, yes, fulfilled, workforce.

The bottom line here is simple. Follow the *Meaning-Centered Leadership* strategies that Barbara and Ed have detailed within, and everyone profits.

Scott Mautz, Speaker and author of *Make It Matter: How Managers Can Motivate by Creating Meaning*

Preface

The constant demand for workplace innovation and the staggering pace of change require organizational leaders to engage, empower, and educate their workforces. Studies have shown time and time again that relationships and employee engagement are critical to the success of the best organizations. This has been demonstrated in the last half-century through the works of researchers like Tom Peters and Robert Waterman of McKinsey and Company; Stephen Covey of Franklin Covey Co., and more recently, Jim Harter and Jim Clifton from Gallup. Unfortunately, according to the 2018 Gallup Poll, 85 percent of the worldwide workforce reports are disengaged.[1] This book offers a research-based leadership approach, *Meaning-Centered Leadership*, that allows leaders to create highly engaged workplaces, thereby increasing the overall performance and profitability of the organization. Leadership devoid of meaning misses the opportunity to optimize workplace outcomes.

The *Meaning-Centered Leadership* approach solves the issue of meaninglessness in the workplace. This book begins with a foundational background on the important impact of creating meaning in the workplace. We succinctly describe the elements of *Meaning-Centered Leadership* supported by recent research. Much has recently been uncovered about the importance of meaning in the workplace to increase employee engagement and satisfaction. *Meaning-Centered Leadership* will provide the how-to of achieving this goal.

Companies are now scrambling to apply the learning to a quickly evolving workplace. In fact, the twenty-first century has brought more meaning-hungry millennials and Gen Z employees into the workforce than ever before. Millennials and Gen Z employees are demanding more meaning and purpose from their workplace. We have concisely reviewed the existing literature on the impact meaning has on health, productivity, and optimal performance for employees and for the organization as a whole. *Meaning-Centered Leadership* presents compelling evidence that exemplary leaders must engage, empower, and educate their followers in ways that foster workplace meaning.

We offer research-based evidence on how leaders can create engaged followers through deep levels of personal engagement. The research conducted with exemplary leaders identified key elements of leadership that lead to deep engagement. Part I of the book describes how leaders use character to build relationships built on trust, care and concern, and open communication with active listening. These relationships are essential for building deep engagement, which in turn leads to workplace meaning.

Part II of the book describes the impact of empowerment on developing workplace meaning. Accordingly, leaders will learn strategies to bring meaning to the everyday struggle of triggering empowerment. Findings are shared on how exemplary leaders use collaborative visioning, recognition, and enthusiasm to create organizational meaning.

In Part III, the book will describe ways in which exemplary leaders use their experience and expertise to develop future-focused followers through wisdom, optimism, and humility. This part also identifies how leaders who express their own personal character and values can influence the overall culture of their organizations.

The final part of the book presents a road map for implementing *Meaning-Centered Leadership* and will bring it all together, supplying leaders with tools to measure meaning and to assess their own personal performance as a meaning-centered leader. This book will lay out strategies and behaviors that will lead to more meaningful leadership, thereby creating a better culture and higher employee engagement. The authors provide clear and actionable behaviors and strategies for leaders to implement immediately to create a workplace filled with meaning.

Finally, the book will offer strategies for leaders to measure workplace meaning so they can assess the impact of their *Meaning-Centered Leadership*. When meaning is created, the overall culture improves and employee engagement will continue to rise. Improved employee engagement will lead to a happier, healthier work environment, which in turn can lead to higher profitability. In short, this book will provide strategies for implementation to create *Meaning-Centered Leadership* in your organization because *meaning matters*!

Acknowledgments

An opportunity of a lifetime presented itself in 2014, when we, Dr. Barbara Bartels and Dr. Edward Jackson, were accepted into the doctoral program at Brandman University, part of the Chapman University System. It was at Brandman that we met Dr. Keith Larick and Dr. Cindy Petersen. Dr. Larick and Dr. Petersen not only supported our dissertation writing but also introduced us to the important research of meaning-making when they invited us, and ten other researchers, to study their meaning-maker concepts.

The theoretical framework they introduced, meaning-makers, was, and continues to be, the focus of important research into how leaders create organizational meaning for themselves and their followers. And the work continues on today as additional researchers have chosen to replicate the original studies and continue the great work started by Dr. Larick and Dr. Petersen.

Dr. Larick and Dr. Petersen's framework, which we used in our research, was foundational to our continued work post-dissertation. Since the completion of our research in early 2017, we have continued our studies together and have developed the *Meaning-Centered Leadership* theory. *Meaning-Centered Leadership* is informed by that meaning-maker research, as well as our combined sixty years of service in education and business, and our continued research on this very important topic.

Initially, we began our research with the meaning-makers with a bit of hesitation, but we soon discovered that the search for meaning is as old as time. Over 2,000 years ago Aristotle claimed that happiness was found in one's work, not in one's pastimes. Thousands of years later, and in agreement with Plato, Socrates, and Aristotle, great philosophers, psychologists, and even recent authors have described a process whereby meaningful work can lead to fulfillment, belongingness, and a deeper sense of purpose. It is against that foundational background that we found ourselves digging deeper into the idea that bringing meaning into the workplace can lead to us to happier, healthier, and more fulfilled lives.

The *Meaning-Centered Leadership* theory we outline in the following pages provides all leaders an easy-to-follow antidote to the aforementioned struggles of organizations filled with meaninglessness, which is all too common in today's environment. This book presents a rich historical overview of the human need for meaning and a compelling call to action for *Meaning-Centered Leadership*.

Introduction

The Case for Meaning

Their chief good and excellence is thought to reside in their work.

—Aristotle

The search for a meaningful life has been a human pursuit for thousands of years, dating back to Ancient Greece through the works of some of the greatest philosophers, including Socrates and Aristotle. Centuries later, psychologists agree, the search for meaning is the primary motivation in one's life. Today, the search for meaning continues and is prevalent not only for individuals but also for organizations.

Current workplace studies have shown high levels of employee disengagement and low levels of employee happiness and satisfaction. Studies have linked happiness, job satisfaction, and employee engagement numbers to organizational profitability. As a result, it is imperative that organizations find ways to improve the employee experience and advance both personal and professional satisfaction.

As people increasingly look to gather deep meaning from their work, organizations must respond with a leadership approach that seeks to develop meaning. *Meaning-Centered Leadership* offers guideposts for leaders to create organizational meaning for themselves and others.

The following chapters will discuss not only the importance of meaning but also strategies and behaviors discovered through the research that exemplary leaders must employ to do just that, instill meaning in the workplace to help increase engagement, empowerment, and employee satisfaction. *Meaning matters!*

Chapter 1

The Seminal Search for Meaning

The quest for meaning has been a fundamental human pursuit since the dawn of time. The search for meaning was documented as early as the advent of philosophy thousands of years ago. Great philosophers like Socrates (469–399 BC), Plato (429–328 BC), and Aristotle (384–322 BC) opined that living well consisted of doing something important and that virtues are activated by lifelong activities. Aristotle said, "Their chief good and excellence is thought to reside in their work." In fact, Plato made his thoughts clear when he defined man: "Man: A being in search of meaning." Plato's works contended that understanding the meaning of life is the greatest form of knowledge. Socrates agreed, saying, "It is not living that matters, but living rightly."

In addition to the seminal works of numerous philosophers seeking meaning, Eastern and Western religious leaders agree that meaning is vital in one's life and the quest for meaning can be fulfilled with one's work. As Buddha (563–483 BC) is said to have stated, "Your purpose in life is to find your purpose and give your heart and soul to it." Later, the human pursuit of purpose and meaning is evidenced in the Old Testament, Micah 6:8, which states "What is good; and what does the Lord require of you but to do justice, and to love kindness, and to walk humbly with your God." Later, Jesus of Nazareth (5 BC–33 AD) spoke much of man's purpose and meaning, as evidenced in many verses, including Matthew 5:16: "Let your light shine before others, that they may see your good deeds and glorify your Father in heaven." And Paul the Apostle states in Romans 8:28, "And we know that for those who love God all things work together for good, for those who are called according to his purpose."

Studies support, as Aristotle stated in ancient Greek philosophy, that the search for meaning is a pursuit not found in pastimes or leisure but in the work in which one is engaged. In fact, Aristotle described happiness as being found in *workings*. Further, religious leaders said that the Earth began because of the work of God; therefore, work must be good because God is good.

Unfortunately, over the years, work has become less of what is good in our lives and more of what must be endured. In fact, in the modern workforce, the division between work hours and time-off is certainly becoming ever increasingly blurred. The advancements of technology have allowed work to transcend deeper in our personal lives, most notably over the past thirty years with the advent of the World Wide Web.

In today's high-tech, highly competitive environment, work oftentimes goes on the road with employees. Cell phones with email access have brought work right into one's living room and even bedroom. Technological advancements have made escaping work seemingly impossible. As a result, when you consider that today most working adults spend the majority of their waking hours at work, or engaging in work-related activities, such as commuting or checking emails, it is more critical than ever to find work that is meaningful and fulfilling.

As we move from ancient philosophers and religious leaders through the centuries, we now take the search for meaning into modern times. In the 1900s psychologists such as Abraham Maslow, Viktor Frankl, Mihaly Csikszentmihalyi, and Martin Seligman agreed when they described the search for meaning as one of the foremost motivations in life. The search for a higher purpose, meaning, and happiness was studied extensively in the mid-1900s and has been at the forefront of more recent discussions on the importance of finding meaning in both our personal and our professional lives.

So, what is this elusive thing called meaning? Meaning is simply developing a sense of value and significance in one's life. Understanding your own personal worth. Meaning is very subjective. What is meaningful to one may not bring meaning to another, but it is this meaning, this fundamental need, to which humans strive to provide fulfillment.

Today, the quest for meaning has not subsided. In fact, the search for meaning is even stronger than ever, especially the search for meaning in the workplace. Research connecting ancient and modern thought leaders creates a clear case for implementing *Meaning-Centered Leadership*, the next great critical leadership theory, founded through the evolution of servant and transformational leadership theories.

In the past decades new approaches to leadership have been suggested by researchers and leadership practitioners. A move away from the transactional leadership approaches of the past has been taking place in the workplace. Many of these leadership theories focused on the dynamics of leader/follower relationships. These theories described how the leader impacted the follower. Transformational leadership, for example, is described as a style of leadership that seeks to fully develop all members of an organization. A transformational leader has been described as a leader who uses inspiration and individual consideration to impact outcomes.

Another leadership approach claims to use wisdom as a basic foundation. Wisdom-based leadership suggests that when leaders use a wise approach, they influence their followers in ways that allow both to flourish. Organizations that use this approach are thought to develop a focus on adding value to society.

Another popular leadership theory that has been around for decades is servant leadership. No theoretical framework is said to exist for servant leadership, but it has been described as the will to lead matched with the need to serve. A servant leader is thought to put the needs of others ahead of their own.

The impact on the follower is central to many of these leadership theories. In authentic leadership, the follower is said to be positively impacted by the leader's ability to create a positive reality for all organizational members. This notion that the leader impacts the reality of the follower is also described as central to the romance of leadership theory. This theory was one of the earliest follower-focused theories. Researchers conclude that leaders have the ability to influence their organizations, in part due to the romanticized impact of the leader.

The impact of the leader was also highlighted in the authentic leadership theory. Researchers have described authentic leadership as having the potential to make a fundamental difference in the organization and in the lives of the followers. The common thread in these leadership approaches is the impact of the leader on their followers.

We believe the greatest impact a leader can have is to create organizational meaning for themselves and their followers. *Meaning-Centered Leadership* is solidly built on many of the ideas espoused in leadership theories of the past several decades that have sought to ameliorate conditions of despair in the modern workplace.

This book will investigate the construct of meaning more deeply and help leaders understand why meaning in the workplace is more critical today than ever before. Understanding the call for meaning, and the meaning-making process, is essential to becoming a meaning-centered leader. The following chapters will provide a clear understanding of the construct of meaning and how it can be implemented in organizations within any sector and of any size. *Meaning-Centered Leadership* must be at the forefront of today's, and tomorrow's, organizations.

Meaning-Centered Leadership has the power to transform the leadership and learning in organizations, whether it is a traditional large business, small business, nonprofit, educational institution, or anything in between. This book will provide the knowledge and skills to help you become a meaning-centered leader. A meaning-centered leader helps others harness the optimal well-being and performance associated with finding meaning in the workplace.

Scott Mautz, author of *Make It Matter: How Managers Can Motivate by Creating Meaning*, illuminated that meaning in the workplace is a necessary solution to disengagement. By engaging employees in meaningful contributions to your organization, you will change the dynamics, success, and happiness throughout the workplace.

This book will focus on describing the importance of *Meaning-Centered Leadership* as a way to improve physical and psychological well-being. It will also provide guidance to show how you, as a leader, can help your followers gain increased meaning from their work. By increasing meaning in the workplace, organizations will experience increased performance and create healthier environments.

MEANING AND EMPLOYEE ENGAGEMENT

In 2018, Gallup released the third *State of the American Workplace* report.[1] Gallup is considered the leader in workforce engagement research with a compilation of over eighty years of research on employee engagement and workforce behaviors. Gallup has interviewed nearly 200,000 employees worldwide and has assessed over 31 million responses to their surveys. Unfortunately, the findings on workforce engagement overall are dismal.

According to the 2018 Gallup Poll results, over 85 percent of workers worldwide report feeling disengaged in their work.[2] How is engagement defined? Engagement can be described as being interested in work, enjoying what you do, putting forth one's best effort at work, and thereby increasing the productivity and success of the organization. Engagement is the key to organizational success and has been the topic of studies by Gallup and others for decades. Unfortunately, the findings in these studies continue to show that engagement over the past few decades has been dismal and, more often than not, declining. Change is imperative if organizations want to thrive.

Truly stop and think about the implications of only 15 percent of the global workforce being fully engaged! The result is not only lower productivity for the organization but simply the fact that there are a lot of unhappy, dissatisfied individuals within these organizations, and that just is not okay. Leaders should be mortified at the fact that their team members are unhappy, especially because it is likely due to poor leadership within the organization and the organizational culture that has been created as a result of ineffective leadership.

In the United States alone, we are faring slightly better than the worldwide statistics. Researchers at Gallup report that 67 percent of workers in the United States can be described as *disengaged* in their work, as compared to the 85 percent worldwide. Unfortunately, this is still a dismal statistic. With

67 percent of U.S. employees being disengaged, this means that only 33 percent of the American workforce is deeply engaged. The U.S. statistics are more than double that of the worldwide statistic, but still nothing to celebrate! If nearly seven out of every ten employees are dissatisfied, imagine what this does to the success of our organizations! It is no surprise with these disheartening figures that America is experiencing declining productivity.

Now let's take a look at the top organizations in the world. What do their engagement figures look like? In the World's Best Organizations, as defined by Gallup, employee engagement is at 70 percent! Remember, worldwide the average workforce engagement level is 15 percent, and in the United States we fare at 33 percent engagement levels. For the world's best organizations, the engagement numbers have flipped to a 70 percent engaged and 30 percent disengaged level. Nearly opposite of the U.S. figures of 33 percent engaged and 67 percent disengaged. Consider how great it would be if America's workforce engagement numbers were flipped!

According to Gallup, organizations classified as the "World's Best Organizations" include USAA, Alliant Credit Union, KinderCare, Hawaii Pacific Health, and many more. The Gallup research has stated that the top organizations have fourteen engaged employees for every one actively disengaged employee – nearly *seven* times the U.S. rate and more than *fifteen times* for workforces globally. Imagine our work lives if every organization could flip the statistic on employee engagement! It's no wonder that over the millennia, work has gone from a source of happiness and an expression of what is good to something that is despised. The disengagement figures show that people simply are not happy at work.

One important aspect to consider when monitoring employee engagement figures is that the quality of life is directly linked to the quality of the working life. If that is the case, the research that points to deep workplace disengagement suggests the vast majority of us experience a far less than optimal quality of life than possible. The impact of this deep dissatisfaction not only impacts the individual worker; it is exponentially passed on to the companies that employ this unhappy workforce, and eventually to the customers which it serves. Decreased engagement leads to decreased productivity, decreased customer satisfaction, and, as a result, decreased profitability. These high levels of disengagement are just bad for business!

Business leaders, researchers, and academic scholars have long studied reasons why workforce engagement is so dismal and has been declining for years. Much of the workforce disengagement can be directly attributed to the leadership team. In fact, leadership is one of the most studied topics, yet it is still one of the most difficult to define and understand. The need to develop improved leadership teams is more important than ever if we are to improve America's engagement and productivity levels.

In 2019, Jim Clifton and Jim Harter of Gallup released the book *It's the Manager*, which is based on the decades of research by the Gallup Polls. Clifton and Harter sum up the research by stating that workforce engagement, or lack thereof, can be directly attributed to the quality of the manager. As a result of the numerous studies on leadership, many leaders have implemented new management strategies in an attempt to increase engagement and employee satisfaction levels.

Other changes we see in today's workplaces include company perks, like gym memberships, flex time, games and activities, free lunches, pets in the workplace, and more. Though nice, research is finding these perks have been developed all in a futile attempt to keep employees engaged. Unfortunately, these perks have not led to sustainable increases in employee engagement figures.

In fact, corporate perks are shown to increase engagement short-term, but it is the culture of the organization which sustains true increases in engagement levels, led by exemplary leaders. Patrick Lencioni and other researchers have shown these perks have increased competition between companies and increased turnover rates. Younger employees are enticed by the perks initially but are leaving jobs at faster rates than ever seen before in hopes of searching for better perks and better satisfaction. Perks are just a temporary fix to a systemic problem of culture and caring. Instead of perks, organizations need to develop a culture of meaning, purpose, and engagement, all vital to developing the workforce of the future, as you will see throughout this book.

So, what makes an exemplary leader exemplary? Much like leadership in general, exemplary leaders have been studied through the years. Research firms like McKinsey & Company and Gallup, as well as scholarly practitioners in leadership and university studies, have studied leadership and how exemplary leaders actually lead. Despite the extensive research conducted over the decades, exemplary leadership skills tend to remain elusive and ever changing. Researchers need to ensure that studies are conducted that actually assess the behaviors and strategies these exemplary leaders use to improve employee engagement. It is the strategies and behaviors that can then be replicated and taught to others to improve upon their leadership skills.

One primary study, foundational to more recent successful leadership practices, dates back to the 1980s when Tom Peters and Robert Waterman, Jr., consultants for the management consulting firm McKinsey & Company, were sent on a mission to find out why the best companies in the United States were successful. Peters and Waterman studied the structure and people side of the business, basically the soft skills and relationship side of business. When Tom Peters and Robert Waterman, Jr., went back to their leadership team with their results, the leaders virtually ignored and set aside the findings. What Peters and Waterman discovered back in the 1980s was simple—employees like to be where they are cared for and respected. Employees are happier when they are engaged, and, perhaps most important, when employees are happy, businesses succeed.

This concept, though rudimentary, was not well received by the leaders at McKinsey & Company. The research was basically dismissed as too "soft" to be a key indicator of success. Tom Peters and Robert Waterman, Jr., believed so deeply in their findings that they published their first, and wildly popular, book in 1982: *In Search of Excellence: Lessons from America's Best Run Companies. In Search of Excellence* was, and continues to be, one of the best-selling business books of all time. It is widely read and often quoted, and Tom Peters is still actively sharing his findings today.

Mark C. Crowley, author of *Lead from the Heart*, conducted a podcast interview on April 14, 2019, with leadership legend Tom Peters. Tom Peters said he continues to discuss his findings, decades later, because he feels that leaders still are not listening to nor implementing the techniques that he discussed nearly forty years ago. In fact, in the podcast, Tom Peters said he is "pissed off" because he is not writing about rocket science. Mr. Peters emphasized that he has been writing about the soft skills for decades! He stressed how saying *please* and *thank you* are vital, saying *sorry* if you screw up is critical, and how just being a decent human being is the key to a successful business leader. Tom Peters expressed his frustration at how, despite the simplicity of the topic, we are still unable to get through to the organizations that so desperately need it. When asked why he continues to repeat the same message, decade after decade, he said he would not give up until organizations "Implement the damn thing!"[3]

Time and time again, authors have written about the soft skills Tom Peters so eloquently recommended decades ago. Based on continuing research and recent Gallup findings, it is readily apparent that leaders are not in touch with the soft skills required for great leadership and great organizations. Tom Peters accentuated how leaders are not managing by wandering/walking around (MBWA) enough. It is vital to get to know the employees, have fun, and really understand people.

Back to the Gallup Poll and the constant news about employee disengagement, it is evident that, although simple to understand and logical to most readers, relationship skills are the most difficult to implement and sustain, yet vital for improved engagement and for creating purpose and meaning in the workplace. *Meaning-Centered Leadership* will help with the implementation of these very needed skills. More importantly, the *Meaning-Centered Leadership* theory will provide strategies and behaviors for execution that can help your organization thrive.

THE *MEANING-CENTERED LEADERSHIP* THEORY

Over the years, numerous leadership theories have been developed, studied, implemented, and changed. Theories come and theories go as organizations change and grow. The evolution of leadership theories has shifted over time with the changing dynamics of the workplace and the workforce. Some earlier leadership theories include the Great Man Theory, Trait Theory, Servant-Leadership, Transactional Leadership, and Transformational Leadership, to name a few. Just look at the Bass and Bass book of leadership theories, and you will begin to understand the significance of the study of leadership.

In today's workplace, it is imperative that leadership practices focus on how leaders can create organizational meaning for themselves and their followers, what we call the *Meaning-Centered Leadership* theory. Authors cite that meaning and purpose improves employee performance and health. On the contrary, meaninglessness has been linked to decreased performance and lowering of the individual's overall health. Today, more than ever, it is critical for leaders to create meaning in their organizations!

In 2002, the preeminent author on servant leadership Robert Greenleaf, speaking of the idealism of the younger generations, said, "They will insist on more determined efforts to provide significant and meaningful work to more people."[4] And sure enough, eighteen years after Robert Greenleaf made his bold statement, the millennial and Gen Z employees are dominating the workforce and proving his statement to be true. Leaders must instill meaning and purpose into employees' work.

There is an urgent need to have leaders who can create meaningful workplaces. This call for meaning in leadership has led to an increased focus on the topic. Focus such as the research we, the authors, participated in at Brandman University. Dr. Keith Larick and Dr. Cindy Petersen led a group of twelve, the meaning-makers, in research to uncover how personal and organizational meaning is created. The researchers studied the behaviors and strategies exemplary leaders use to create meaning within their organization. Each researcher in the thematic study identified exemplary leaders from numerous industries, from CEOs to technology leaders, superintendents of K–12 schools to university presidents, police chiefs, and more. Since 2017, more researchers have continued to be interested in this topic. The study has been replicated a few more times, adding depth to the findings through studying small business owners and special education administrators. The results are unanimous. In all organizations at all levels, *meaning matters!*

Meaning can have a profound influence on organizational performance as well as on an individual's health and well-being. The research concludes that a *Meaning-Centered Leadership* approach could provide an elixir to all those voiceless survey participants who have concluded their work has little to no meaning, stating how they suffer because of it. In fact, a *Meaning-Centered Leadership* approach could, and should, be applied in all sectors of industries, from education to business to nonprofit work. Just as businesses have begun to embrace the transformative power of meaning, leaders from all industries need a framework for creating meaning. This book provides that framework.

With the foundational justification for meaning in the workplace covered, let's take a deeper look at the elusive search for meaning through time. Why have people been so interested in meaning and how does it impact the lives of humans?

THE TIMELESS SEARCH CONTINUES

Researchers throughout the years have studied philosophers and religious leaders, and it is evident that the search for meaning dates back centuries. Man has been in search of meaning since the dawn of time. *What is the meaning of life?* is an age-old question with very elusive and ever-changing answers. As discussed earlier, philosophers such as Plato, Socrates, Aristotle, and their contemporaries seemingly insisted that virtuous activity is the highest good and that virtuous toil would lead an individual to a fulfilled life. Meaning has been studied by these philosophers dating back centuries, and yet this topic has not been brought into the workplace until the last few decades.

So, let us bring the quest for meaning to current times. Contemporary philosophers and psychologists share the idea that meaningful work can lead a person to a meaningful life. Some have said that finding meaning is a fundamental human right and the very essence of human existence. And today, more than ever, there is a renewed search for meaning, both in personal and professional lives. Meaning in the workplace is increasingly popular with university researchers and business gurus. As we see workplace engagement suffer, the need to find meaning is even more important than ever. The search for meaning is truly timeless.

Viktor Frankl (1905–1977), a renowned psychologist and Holocaust survivor, informed much of the modern thought about the creation of personal meaning. Frankl was an Austrian neurologist and psychologist before he and his family became prisoners in a Nazi internment camp. While interned, Frankl lost his wife and children at the hands of Hitler's regime. Despite his deplorable conditions, Viktor continued to find meaning in his situation, including seeking simple moments of purpose, such as sneaking a small piece of potato in his pocket or finding a moment to speak with other prisoners to challenge them to survive by finding meaning in their situation.

Frankl was the founder of the cognitive-behavioral therapy practice he titled *logotherapy* (*logos* is the Greek word for meaning), which states the primary motivation of humans is to find meaning in life. Frankl's work was foundational to the study of meaning-making in the modern world. Upon his release, Frankl authored the book *Man's Search for Meaning* in 1946, which has sold over 12 million copies. Through his experiences and his work in psychiatry, Frankl observed the search for meaning as a primary driver of seeking purpose in one's life, and it can be seen in his quote, "Man's search for meaning is the primary motivation in his life and not a secondary rationalization of instinctual drives." Frankl further insisted, "What man actually needs is not a tensionless state but rather the striving and struggling for a worthwhile goal, a freely chosen task."[5] For the past eighty-plus years, Frankl's book remains one of the most important works in today's understanding of the search for meaning.

Following Frankl, Mihaly Csikszentmihalyi described work as the marker of a healthy culture. To keep a society healthy, productive, and moving forward, healthy work environments must be a priority. In his 1990 book *Flow: The Psychology of Optimal Experience*, Csikszentmihalyi explained that when one finds flow in work and relationships, it can lead to an improved quality of life. "The consequence of forging a life by purpose and resolution is a sense of inner harmony, a dynamic order in the contents of consciousness."[6] Csikszentmihalyi suggested that as long as people view work as the Curse of Adam, finding satisfaction in this important part of life will be difficult.

When we triangulate the data from all the research on meaning and living a meaningful life, and we add in research on employee engagement, or lack thereof, we find that most employees, unfortunately, do, in fact, view work as the Curse of Adam. This is the reason employees are disengaged in work today. The majority of the workforce, as seen in the Gallup research outlined previously, view work as simply something to be endured, something that just has to happen to survive.

Csikszentmihalyi theorized that the path to personal satisfaction lies in learning how to create enjoyment in what happens every day, which is the goal of *Meaning-Centered Leadership*. He stated, "The best moments in our lives are not the passive, receptive, relaxing times. . . . The best moments usually occur if a person's body or mind is stretched to its limits in a voluntary effort to accomplish something difficult and worthwhile."[7] *Meaning-Centered Leadership* is designed to help create increased opportunities for individuals to experience enhanced work/life satisfaction and create everyday enjoyment by helping people to see that the work they do is, in fact, worthwhile!

Moving ahead a few decades, in his 2011 book, *Flourish: A Visionary New Understanding of Happiness and Well-Being*, Martin Seligman described his well-being theory. The goal of the theory is to increase the level of flourishing by increasing positive emotion and relationships, while increasing accomplishment, engagement, and meaning. His theory singles out meaning as clearly one of the foundations of well-being. As such, it is essential that individuals experience meaning in their personal and professional lives.

Meaningful work was also the topic of business leader and author Scott Mautz's 2015 book *Make It Matter*. Mautz illustrated how meaning could be created at work. He also cited the Gallup research, describing the widespread disengagement at work. Speaking less about engagement and more about satisfaction, surveys found that less than 50 percent of Americans are satisfied with their jobs. Stop for a second and imagine how this impacts each and every organization—from the nonprofits, to publicly traded for-profit business, to the small mom and pop shops, to the K–12 classroom! If less than 50 percent of all employees are not satisfied, this is clear evidence that organizations are not concerned about their employees. It is time to improve not only engagement scores but also overall job satisfaction levels. All leaders in all organizations can be positively impacted by meaning, or negatively impacted by meaninglessness.

And finally, bringing the search for meaning in the workplace to today, two new books were recently released. Author and business consultant Jeff Kofman released his book *The Meaning Revolution: The Power of Transcendent Leadership*, in 2018, where he discussed how it is imperative leaders bring meaning to the workplace. And most recently, in 2019, a new book from Gallup by Jim Clifton and Jim Harter, *It's the Manager*, clearly and succinctly states that today's workforce clearly cares less about the paycheck and more about the purpose of working for a particular organization. Clifton and Harter, as well as many other authors, imply that it is the responsibility of leaders (coaches) in the organization to help employees find their why, their meaning, their reason for giving all they've got to the organization, not only for the organization but for a higher purpose.

The *Meaning-Centered Leadership* theory is here to help leaders transform how others experience work. The *Meaning-Centered Leadership* approach will change the paradigm of meaningless work into something that is meaningful and an important contribution to the workplace, society, and the world. The workforce of the twenty-first and twenty-second centuries will most certainly demand this change.

Research continues to support that the future of leadership requires a commitment to the people side of the house, the soft skills, per se! Perhaps, decades later, Tom Peters may just get his wish as we define clear and specific strategies for implementing *Meaning-Centered Leadership* in the workplace.

Chapter 2

The Impact of Meaning

> Once an individual's search for meaning is successful, it not only renders him happy but also gives him the capability to cope with suffering.
>
> —Viktor Frankl, *Man's Search for Meaning*

In this chapter we will provide the case for developing meaning in the workplace and the positive impact it can create within your workforce. Meaning matters because people are craving meaning, significance, and purpose in their lives. It is essential to the health and well-being of individuals and the organizations for which they work. The goal is to seek this higher level of significance and purpose. As seen in the quote above by Viktor Frankl, finding meaning allows a person the ability to deal with both victory and defeat more effectively.

Today, more than ever, the most basic needs are met for most working adults. Basic needs include food, water, and shelter. Think back to 1943 with Abraham Maslow's Human Motivation Theory. Maslow demonstrated his Hierarchy of Needs model through the picture of a pyramid. Maslow's theory stated one tier of the pyramid must be met for a person to be motivated enough to move to the next level of the pyramid. Maslow ultimately stated that humans have the innate desire to reach the top of the pyramid, to achieve self-actualization, where meaning and purpose are found. Humans have the inborn desire to be all that they can be, and further, to have a purpose for living.

The first level of the pyramid reflects physiological needs. Physiological needs are foundational to existence, and typically, these needs are met at the primary ages after birth. These basic human physiological needs include food, water, and the ability to rest to sustain our most basic existence.

Without these needs being met, one cannot survive. Once these most basic needs are consistently met, an individual is able to move to the second level of the pyramid.

The second level of the pyramid is what Maslow terms as safety needs. Safety needs include emotional safety, psychological safety, and personal safety. Examples of safety needs include security for your well-being, a roof over your head, and emotional stability. Financial security is also an important component of the second level of the pyramid. Again, in today's workforce, most employees are able to attain this second level of basic human needs, so they are ready to move on to level three.

The third level is that of belongingness and love. For an individual to survive, they must feel a sense of belonging and love. Humans need love. Love can come from family, friends, the workplace, and social groups. It is at this level where people get involved in sports teams or different clubs and activities. People spend time with family and friends in social settings. Without a sense of belongingness, in some form or another, a person may suffer from depression, loneliness, and anxiety. One must feel some sense of belongingness to move to the next level. Feelings of belongingness and love differ for every individual and can come from different sources, but without them, according to Maslow, one cannot fully move to the fourth level.

The fourth level of Maslow's Hierarchy of Needs pyramid is one of self-esteem. Self-esteem develops when one feels accomplished and respected. The ego comes into play at the fourth level of the pyramid. Humans must feel esteem both internally and externally. People thrive when they are confident and proud of themselves. A person must have self-respect, as well as external respect, which develops through the recognition and validation from others. People must feel valued for what they do. It is here where people start to consider their contribution to the world. It is here where the workplace can support a person's goal and be supportive of the development of this level. Without self-esteem, a person may suffer from feelings of inferiority, which can slide them right back to the emotional safety needs. By developing self-esteem, though, it does not mean that an individual becomes a narcissist, or arrogant; it just means that they are on their way to seeking the meaning and purpose in their life, which is the top tier of the pyramid, level five.

Most people who are in the workforce today have food, shelter, clothing, friends, and perhaps even a sense of accomplishment and a positive self-esteem, but what they are now seeking is meaning and purpose—the top tier of the pyramid—self-actualization. The creation of meaning helps to set the stage for presenting the antidote to disengagement and low performance—*Meaning-Centered Leadership*.

Self-actualization allows a person to have the confidence to continue to self-reflect, learn, and grow so that they meet their full potential. A person who has reached this level of the pyramid has reached self-actualization. Some leaders who state they have reached level five say they are doing exactly what they were put on earth to do. They love what they do and they do what they love.

Everyone's self-actualization levels may look different. Some feel they have reached this level through the way in which they raise their children. Others may find their self-actualization through their work—being the absolute best they can be in the position that they love and enjoy. Others may find it in their volunteer positions or an activity in which they participate. Again, it does not matter where the meaning is found; what is important is that all people have the opportunity to find it. It is here where one is confident, comfortable, happy, and more importantly, filled with a sense of meaning and purpose.

In today's environment, it is critical that organizations help their employees be engaged and seek meaning in their daily work. This will ensure the vitality of the organization for the long term. Let's take a deeper look into the importance of meaning in your organization and the negative impact that occurs when there is a lack of meaning.

In their 2010 book, *The Why of Work*: *How Great Leaders Build Abundant Organizations That Win*, Dave and Wendy Ulrich made a compelling case for leaders to build meaning to better serve their followers. Like many of the other authors in the research, Dave and Wendy Ulrich agree that when people have meaningful work, they are able to find meaning in life.

Meaning is also essential to workplace engagement. Meaning at work has been linked to improved employee performance and improved health. Additionally, satisfying work experiences are important for individuals and for the organizations in which they work. There is an immediate need for leaders who can foster meaning for their employees. Through finding meaningful work, a person can find a sense of purpose, belonging, and fulfillment.

Almost everyone can relate to stories that articulate how leaders have failed to engage others due to practices that failed to create meaning for the follower. We know this by the dismal employee engagement numbers discussed previously. It seems there are daily examples and announcements about poor leadership. Talk to just about anyone you know who is employed and ask if they have a story about an ineffective leader. Ask for specific examples and you are sure to hear things like: *They don't value me. They don't care about me. They don't know me. They create a toxic work environment. They don't listen. They simply are not kind. They don't like people!* The list is endless.

Though the search for meaning is an age-old quest, the topic of finding meaning and purpose in the workplace is a fairly recent discussion. Meaning has had more attention as the engagement levels have declined and people are striving to reach the top tier of self-actualization on Maslow's pyramid.

Meaning is a must for businesses that want to heighten performance and maximize profits while creating a healthier workplace. On the contrary, meaninglessness has been seen to decrease performance and impede health.

As we discussed in chapter 1, according to the 2018 Gallup Poll *State of the American Workplace*, only 33 percent of employees in America stated feeling engaged at work, and worse, across 142 countries, only 15 percent of employees stated feeling engaged at work. Study participants defined work as a depleting, dispiriting experience, and it may be getting worse. Furthermore, looking beyond just engagement, numerous studies have demonstrated a decline in satisfaction and happiness in the workplace. Employees today have not only been less engaged than their colleagues in the decades prior but also dissatisfied and unhappy.

But there is a small glimmer of hope. After years of continuous decline, it is good to know that the engagement numbers have increased ever so slightly in the past five years, albeit by a small amount. There was a slight 3 percent increase in employee engagement in the United States from 2013 to 2018, yet the numbers remain dismal. Employee engagement must continue to increase if there is hope to make an impact on the steadily decreasing American productivity statistics. If U.S. organizations do not make a change in engagement levels, the impact of disengagement will be the demise of American productivity. Leaders within organizations must make a significant and disruptive change in the way they treat their employees. After all, happy employees lead to happy customers, which, in turn, leads to happy and profitable organizations.

All organizations should be striving for a 180-degree shift in employee engagement, seeking the goal of a 70 percent engagement level instead of a 30 percent engagement level. Unfortunately, there is a long way to go to change the engagement numbers to match those of the Best Worldwide Organizations! According to Gallup, the Best Worldwide Organizations are riding at a 70 percent positive employee engagement, proving that it truly is possible to have happy, healthy, and engaged employees!

Imagine if all organizations had 70 percent of their employees fully engaged. Engaged employees have higher job satisfaction with increased productivity and effectiveness, thereby increasing productivity and overall profitability. As a result, keeping employees happy and satisfied positively impacts the overall success of the organization. It is time to instill *Meaning-Centered Leadership* to increase engagement levels of our workforce today. Even if we could only double the American workforce engagement numbers from a 33 percent engagement level to a 66 percent engagement level, organizations would be making a world of difference on the impact of employee well-being, as well as on the production levels as a byproduct of this increased engagement.

In fact, 181 of the top executives agree—*meaning matters!* On August 19, 2019, a group of 181 CEOs signed a Business Roundtable pledge acknowledging the role that businesses play in helping their employees experience meaning. In part, their statement reads, "Americans deserve an economy that allows each person to succeed through hard work and creativity and to lead a life of meaning and dignity. . . . we share a fundamental commitment to all our stakeholders."[1] This is a shift from the idea that the company serves the shareholders first and foremost. The pledge goes on to state that the leaders acknowledge their companies' role in helping their workforce develop the skills required in a rapidly changing workplace. They declared their intention to create workplaces that valued promoting dignity and respect for their employees.

Meaning-Centered Leadership provides the template for delivering on that promise. By focusing on the important leadership elements presented in our book, leaders at all levels will be able to deliver on the pledge endorsed by these CEOs. Each and every worker in our economy deserves the opportunity to experience dignity and meaning at work and *Meaning-Centered Leadership* will help develop the leaders of tomorrow.

Rich Karlgaard, the publisher of *Forbes*, says the next cycle of business must include Meaning, purpose, and deep life experience. As noted, meaning, purpose, and fulfillment increase employee engagement and satisfaction, which studies contend will translate to increases in the bottom line. As Thomas Moore references in his 2008 book *A Life at Work: The Joy of Discovering What You Were Born to Do*, "People want to engage in work that gives their lives meaning and they want to do work that is ethical and contributes to society as a whole."[2] On average, a full-time employee spends more than one-third of their waking life preparing for work or conducting tasks for which they are paid, so it is critical that one finds a career that provides meaning. Research shows that the need for meaning in the workplace is on the rise, and we must find clear and specific ways in which to increase a meaningful work environment.

RETURN ON INVESTMENT

If you are the financial guru in your organization, you rely on the return on investment (ROI) numbers. Of course, for a business to sustain, all stakeholders should be concerned with ROI, so let's talk about the impact of meaning on the ROI of your organization. This proves we are not talking just *fluff*—the soft skills, as some skeptics like to say. Meaning has a clear and measurable ROI, which means increases to the overall profitability of your organization.

For the health of an organization to be sustained in the twenty-first century, it is imperative to ensure that employees are finding meaning in their work. As we have seen, increasing a sense of meaningfulness at work is one of the most powerful ways to increase engagement and performance. Research also shows when employees obtain meaning from their work, they are more than three times as likely to stay with their organizations. This statistic surely impacts your bottom line! An organization's workforce is what makes or breaks an organization's success. By creating a meaningful organization, the retention factor alone will save organizations millions of dollars.

In today's workforce, two of the most pressing issues are employee retention and employee recruitment, as we will discuss below. According to Gallup, U.S. businesses are losing one trillion dollars per year due to voluntary employee turnover. Yes, you saw that correctly—*trillion* with a *t*. In fact, according to the 2017 Labor Statistics, the turnover rate in the United States is over 26 percent annually.

It is estimated that employee turnover can cost a business between one half to two times the salary when an employee leaves the organization. To put this in dollar figures, if you have 100 employees, the average salary is $50,000 and you experience a 26 percent turnover rate, the cost to rehire could be as low as $650,000 or as high as $2.5 million dollars![3] And this calculation is for organizations with only 100 employees. This is considered a small business. The dollars lost increases exponentially with larger organizations. Imagine the savings within the great companies that sustain a 70 percent engagement rate. The World's Best Organizations are saving millions of dollars annually just because they are able to recruit the best and, more importantly, they are able to retain them.

Think back to the statistic stated above: *A person is three times more likely to stay if there is meaning in the workplace*. This is impactful! Create meaning. Give your employees a reason to stay. Spot check your organization in an honest assessment of recruitment, retention, and leadership. Review department by department. If you see high turnover rates in any particular division, analyze why and fix it. Studies show it is likely due to the manager. People stay with leaders because they love working with them. Similarly, people leave an organization because of their leaders. Your organization may have a very bright leader, but if the turnover is high, do an honest assessment of whether the leader aligns with the values and ethics that form your organization. If your findings are that the leader cannot be coached with all that we share in the remainder of this book, it's time to let that leader go!

The retention cost dollar figures address the costs of advertising, rehiring, training, and onboarding, but there are also many hidden costs that cannot be directly accounted for when someone leaves. If you are losing a star performer or top producer, you could be losing much more than just the costs related to hiring and training the next employee. When a star performer leaves, you may also lose some of your top customers. Your star performers have established strong relationships and ties to their customers, so you are risking the customer following your star performer right out the door.

Further, if you lose a star performer, you are also likely losing an individual who required less managing, was more innovative, and was more productive overall. In addition, if you are losing a well-liked individual, the other team members may consider leaving. In fact, studies have shown that more than half of the employees who leave were searching for new positions for months prior to their departure, which clearly leads to decreased engagement. The person job-hunting is clearly less engaged, likely even searching for a job on the web from their desk!

Studies have also shown that while the star performer was job searching, more often than not, not one of their leaders or people in management had spoken to them about their future with the organization or even if they were satisfied in their position. Not surprisingly, some of those interviewed said they might have stayed if management had asked about them or showed some care and concern. This means that, had some crucial and authentic conversations taken place on a regular basis, the leader may have been able to intervene and thereby avoid some key resignations. A meaning-centered leader would recognize the employee dissatisfaction and address it and discuss it with the goal of preventing departures of key employees.

The other dangerous result of high turnover rates is the fact that people talk to each other. Employees admitted that they made it known to other colleagues that they were seeking a new position elsewhere, which can clearly have an impact on the team. Team members may begin to internalize and question why they are staying if the top performer is leaving. The gossip mill begins to swirl, employees make speculations, and the negativity begins. The downward spiral of decreased inspiration, motivation, morale, and happiness can happen quickly when a star member of a team leaves. An aftereffect of a top performer leaving can be detrimental as others may follow suit and also leave. This snowball effect, and the actual money lost as a result, is why retention is vital to the health of an organization's team and overall health of the organization. Creating a meaningful workplace is vital to retention.

Lack of meaning leads to lack of engagement, which leads to increased absenteeism. People take unscheduled work days off because they are sick, disengaged, unappreciated, unmotivated, frustrated, stressed, or even depressed. According to one study by Gallup-Healthways Well-Being Index, the total costs due to unscheduled absenteeism exceed $84 billion annually. The cost includes lost wages, which ranges from $2,500 for salaried employees to $3,600 on average for hourly employees, as well as having to pay other employees overtime or having to hire temporary personnel to fill in the gaps. The problem increases exponentially because having people absent leads to extra work and undue stress to other employees. Even if a temporary person is hired, the temp will not have the knowledge or training that a full-time employee would have; therefore, the stress on other employees increases. Absenteeism leads to a vicious cycle of increased disengagement and decreased meaning in the workplace.

Additional research reported by the Gallup business journal found that managers who are focused on engagement will inevitably increase productivity. High levels of engagement lead to 22 percent higher profitability and 21 percent higher productivity. The report added that turnover is 65 percent lower in highly engaged workplaces and customer ratings exceed low engagement workplaces by 10 percent. Managers who focus on creating engagement develop deep interpersonal relationships with their followers, and they are involved in their employees' work lives. Followers who meet regularly with their managers generate higher performance and are more likely to report that someone cares about them. In addition, they have triple the level of engagement over followers who do not meet regularly with their managers. Higher engagement leads to higher productivity and happiness.

In summary, there most certainly is a direct cost and return on investment in keeping your employees happy, healthy, and fulfilled. Take care of your employees to decrease the costs associated with recruitment, retention, and absenteeism. *Meaning-Centered Leadership* is the vaccine that can help prevent some of the very costly ailments that come with meaninglessness.

HAPPINESS AND WELL-BEING

Finding meaning allows employees to feel good about what they are doing, which in turn motivates them to increase productivity. Without meaning, happiness and well-being may suffer. Through a leader's ability to create connections with employees, and then to recognize and appreciate the effort and attention an employee puts into their work, a follower will feel their work means more and the organization will benefit.

When leaders and organizations work with a high standard of values and ethics, employees are able to put forth their best efforts and aspirations. In fact, as early as 1989, a study by positive psychology guru Mihaly Csikszentmihalyi reported that employees who experienced more flow at work than in their leisure time were more active, alert, focused, happy, and satisfied. Basically, Csikszentmihalyi validates that well-being is impacted through meaning. In his book *Flow: The Psychology of Optimal Achievement*, Csikszentmihalyi stated, "We are biologically programmed to find other human beings the most important objects in the world."[4]

Similar to Maslow's belongingness and love, Csikszentmihalyi explained that people's happiness depends on how they manage their relationships with others. He elaborated that when an individual does find their flow in the work they do and the relationships they build with others, they will have a better quality of life overall. He later added, "The sooner we realize that the quality of the work experience can be transformed at will, the sooner we can improve this enormously important dimension of life."[5] Csikszentmihalyi, like Tom Peters, recognized the importance of relationships, flow, and the need for soft skills so employees could feel more satisfaction in their daily lives. Many authors and researchers in the 1980s were looking at these traits and desperately seeking implementation of these soft skills, yet decades of declining employee satisfaction followed, validating Tom Peters' comments that organizations just are not implementing these skills.

Decades after Csikszentmihalyi published his research, the information was further validated when Martin Seligman, the leader of the positive psychology movement, described relationships as being fundamental to well-being. He explains that the prefrontal cortex is a machine that functions to facilitate effective human relationships. In 2004, Martin Seligman participated in a TedTalk where he described positive psychology and the way in which psychology has changed over the years. Through positive psychology, the goal is to make miserable people less miserable, but also to make happier people experience even more happiness.

Seligman describes three types of lives: the pleasant life, the good life, and the meaningful life. A pleasant life consists of positive emotions and people using these emotions to make themselves better and happier on a more consistent basis. A good life is better than a pleasant life, and a person in this stage experiences more flow, whereby time stops when they are doing exactly what they love. Finally, a meaningful life focuses on the strengths of an individual and how they use their strengths to impact more than just their own life but also the lives of others. Like Maslow's theory, a meaningful life is where self-actualization takes place. Further, Seligman also postulates that the more social a person is, the happier they are overall. Positive relationships thrive with happier individuals.

Happiness and well-being can be a choice, as noted by numerous studies on human psychology, and it most certainly can be supported through the leader's ability to motivate and inspire the team. Studies show that the time, energy, and effort to help people find meaning in work makes them appreciate their work more while providing an increased sense of ownership. Lack of meaning leads to lack of ownership. Lack of ownership affects the bottom line of the organization, as was shared in the "Return on Investment" section.

Ownership can be encouraged by management through allowing an employee to create and pave the way to success in their own position. Scott

Mautz, author of *Make It Matter: How Managers Can Motivate by Creating Meaning*, said that humans are deeply fulfilled and energized when their work has deep significance and value. People prosper when they feel they are doing what they were *meant* to be doing. Dan Aierly, professor of psychology and behavioral economics at Duke University, calls this the *Ikea Effect*, which proves that when one puts time and effort into work to build something great, it has more meaning.

A good leader can support and encourage creativity and meaning by allowing flexibility and the freedom to decide how to get to the end result. This freedom will make the task more meaningful when it is accomplished. By building opportunities for increased meaning and fulfillment, leaders can develop employees who see value and importance in their work. More importantly, studies theorize that feelings of accomplishment, respect, and meaning in the workplace are more powerful motivators for coming to work than the paycheck received. The potential for a trickle-down negative impact on meaning is far too great to not get all this right.

Throughout the research, employees made comments about micromanagement and the inefficiencies it causes. The phrase *paralysis by analysis* was heard over and over again. People want to know that they can be trusted to get their job done without management monitoring every move, such as how many calls or emails they sent that week. Employees want the flexibility to know the desired result and appreciate the leadership team that gives them the flexibility to reach the final goal. It is critically important to provide clarity on the end goal, the why, with less importance on the steps needed to reach the end goal, the how. Distrust leads to disengagement and micromanaging the how leads to mistrust. This level of leadership breeds trust and transparency and helps more team members to be star performers. Leaders must trust that employers know the *how* to get the *what* done efficiently and effectively.

Skunk Works, a division of Lockheed Martin founded in 1943, is a prime example of an organization that allows creativity and disruptive innovation to take place, especially while searching for new and innovative developments. Leadership at Skunk Works is known to provide an extreme level of autonomy to its employees. In addition, creativity is encouraged through the ability to make mistakes and the freedom to innovate, all leading to technologies no one knew existed. Trust that the organization has hired smart-enough people that know how to do their jobs, provided they know the desired end result and that they have the appropriate tools to complete the task.

Other examples of the payback from autonomy to innovate are well known. Take Google's 20 percent time that founders Larry Paige and Sergey Bren claimed led to increased creativity and innovation and allegedly to Google News, Gmail, and AdSense. It is this type of creativity and innovation that launched the humble but wildly popular sticky note for 3M. Creativity and autonomy create meaning in the workplace and also open up the opportunity for great success to the bottom line.

Research shows a clear link between meaning and well-being. Organizations with engaged employees experience positive business performance, while workplaces with disengaged employees are more likely to experience lower productivity. According to the World Health Organization, depression is the most costly disease in the world. On average, treating a case of depression costs $5,000 per year. Sadly, there are around 10 million such cases of depression logged annually in America. Depression could lead to increased absenteeism, and as previously demonstrated, absenteeism is costly to organizations. Decreasing stress leads to a lower likelihood of developing depression. It is imperative that organizations increase meaning to buffer the negative effects of stress.

So how do organizations decrease work-related stress? Research overwhelmingly supports organizational investment in leadership. The demanding and complex nature of leadership can leave leaders feeling drained of the resources they need. Leaders need to be mindful that they have sufficient emotional bandwidth to care for their followers. When a leader is drained, anxiety has an opportunity to replace optimism and their ability to lead effectively is greatly diminished. Throughout our book we offer tips and strategies to help leaders maintain their own personal reservoirs of meaning. When leading from this fully charged perspective, leaders will have an increased ability to deliver the complex array of skills and strategies needed to bolster organizational meaning.

Organizations and leaders also need to be aware that research suggests that the majority of workplace-related depressive episodes are connected to leader-follower relationships. Bullying and mistreatment in the workplace are largely attributed to the leader. Longitudinal research suggests that when employees experience workplace bullying, their mental health can be substantially impacted. Clearly, a bullying boss is the antithesis of a meaning-centered leader; however, this research shows the compelling impact that leadership can have on employee mental health. By following the *Meaning-Centered Leadership* approach, leaders will not only be able to recharge their personal reservoirs of meaning; they will be able to focus on the important elements of leadership that lead to workplace meaning for their followers.

Investing in leadership training and support has the opportunity to develop individuals in the organization. When leaders are fully resourced and optimistic, they will impart that to their followers. They will be able to focus on the important elements of leadership outlined in this book—elements that can make the difference between performance and the engagement associated with an organization that is full of meaning.

Organizations must start with ensuring their leaders are adequately prepared to engage in the processes outlined in this book. The process of engagement leads to the creation of workplace meaning. With leadership fully prepared to engage in *Meaning-Centered Leadership* practices, organizations can turn their attention to organizational practices that support the development of meaning—practices that show the organization is concerned with the well-being of their community. The following vignette from the research demonstrates how organizational meaning can be built outside of the workplace.

One respondent in our research discussed how their organization develops teamwork, happiness, and well-being through community service days. These days do not have to be taken as sick days, nor do they have to be taken as vacation days. Volunteerism, and doing good for the community and others, is something the organization recognizes and encourages. This volunteerism creates happiness for those serving and also for those being served. Meaning is instilled outside the workplace and meaning is created within the employees and organization itself. It is a win-win situation for all parties involved.

The impact of meaning in the workplace is significant. Meaning increases engagement. Organizations that struggle to create meaning experience higher costs in recruitment and retention, and higher costs due to increased stress and absenteeism. The return on investment is evident. Increased engagement decreases turnover rates and decreases absenteeism. Meaning decreases stress, which thereby increases happiness and well-being. Studies support the importance of increased meaning and fulfillment in the workplace. Creating a culture in which employees find meaning and purpose in their work is critical for the health and well-being of the individuals, as well as the organization. The future success of organizations depends on it. Leaders within organizations have a responsibility to ensure the work environments support opportunities to create meaning. *Meaning-Centered Leadership* implementation can potentially save organizations millions of dollars in the long run. Just look at the research! Invest in your leaders and invest in your people. Develop a meaning-centered approach, and success will follow.

Chapter 3

The Elements of
Meaning-Centered Leadership

Meaningful workplaces have values-based organizational cultures that
consider employees just as important as customers, if not more so.

—Neal Chalofsky, *Meaningful Workplaces*

Meaning-Centered Leadership provides the antidote needed to resolve issues
related to lack of engagement and meaninglessness in organizations today. If
a person finds a sense of purpose, belonging, and fulfillment, they can find
meaning in their work. This chapter presents a clear overview of the new
leadership model, *Meaning-Centered Leadership*, including the three elements of being a meaning-centered leader: engagement, empowerment, and
expertise.

The *Meaning-Centered Leadership* approach provides a clear path for
leaders to maximize their ability to increase engagement and to become a
leader who focuses on creating meaning within their organization. In this
chapter, the three elements of *Meaning-Centered Leadership*—engagement,
empowerment, and expertise—are presented. These elements were found
throughout the research on how exemplary leaders and their followers experience the process of gathering meaning from their work, validated in the
research discussed in the previous chapters.

- *Engagement* through building trust, showing care and concern, and practicing open communication with active listening are essential first steps in
becoming a meaning-centered leader.
- *Empowerment* through collaborative visioning, recognition, and enthusiasm is another essential element of creating an environment filled with
meaning.

- *Expertise* expressed as wisdom, defined as experience grounded by principles, optimism for the future, and humility, must all be used by meaning-centered leaders.

The imperative of these three elements for creating meaning was not only voiced by the participants in our research; it is also reflected throughout the literature on the impact of meaning on the workplace. These three elements are essential components of provisioning meaning, but they do not exist in isolation. It is vital that all three elements be present for a leader to become an exemplary meaning-centered leader. One element is simply not enough to meet the needs of the employees striving for a meaningful workplace. A leader who has high levels of engagement and yet does not empower their employees to be the best they can be will find employee engagement nearly impossible to sustain for the long term. All three elements must be working concurrently and consistently to maintain the meaning-centered approach.

Engagement, empowerment, and expertise will be presented in separate sections, but you will see the constant interplay of all three elements. Throughout our research we found that a clear vision for the future helps followers develop engagement, but it is the leader/follower engagement that provides an avenue for sharing that vision. For that reason, engagement is seen as an essential first step in becoming a meaning-centered leader. Research has found that when leaders build a foundational relationship built on trust with each of their followers, they deepen engagement.

We see this same interplay of the elements of creating meaning when discussing empowerment. Without the open communication of engagement, it will be nearly impossible for empowerment to take place. The collaborative visioning found in empowerment must be informed by a future-focused orientation expressed by the leader's expertise.

Lastly, expertise expressed through wisdom, optimism, and humility cannot exist if the leader is unable to openly communicate to employees, while motivating and empowering them to be the best they can be. In this constant interplay, it is easy to lose sight of your leadership focus. We offer the meaning-centered lens on leadership as a way to keep your focus on what is most important: *meaning!*

"When we find meaning in our work, we find meaning in life."

—Dave and Wendy Ulrich, *The Why of Work*

It is essential that a leader creates a systematic approach that includes each of the elements of *Meaning-Centered Leadership* in their day-to day-work. The three elements provide an organizing framework for identifying, measuring, and focusing on meaningful leadership work. As each element is presented in the coming chapters, we will offer strategies for developing processes and procedures to ensure engagement, empowerment, and expertise remain a focus of a leader's daily work.

Shifts in behavior and intentional practice will allow a leader to maximize their skills in leading with meaning. Again, this is not difficult, but it must be practiced regularly. In addition, examples will be provided that demonstrate meaningfulness through positive leadership, as well as how meaninglessness can develop through poor leadership. These examples are common and unfortunately seen more often than desired in today's workforce, leading to the poor employee engagement and productivity figures previously discussed.

In later chapters, we will share tools for measuring each of the elements. Peter Drucker once wrote: "What gets measured gets managed." The measurement tools we offer in chapter 14 provide a great way to quantify your impact as you incorporate and refine your *Meaning-Centered Leadership* elements. It is imperative to get feedback from those impacted by your leadership. It is also important to note that measurement tools provide an opportunity for reflection and refinement, but it is the day-to-day focus on the framework that will allow you to deepen meaning for yourself and your followers, so you can become a meaning-centered leader.

We believe the simplicity of the framework will allow all adherents of the meaning-centered approach to focus on the core elements on a regular basis. In each section we will offer immediate success strategies that were either demonstrated by the exemplary leaders that were interviewed or discussed time and time again in the literature. Further, each section contains reflective strategies for examining your current practice, including activities and examples designed to deepen your understanding of how you engage, empower, and use your expertise to create meaning.

We began this book by describing the concept of meaning and the impact, or lack thereof, that meaning has on individuals and organizations. Before you begin Part I, it is imperative that you do so prepared for change. We encourage you to view your work through the lens of *Meaning-Centered Leadership*. We believe that lens will allow you to maximize your potential to deeply impact others, transcend the ordinary, and transform your work environment.

It is also important to note the definition of a leader. A leader is someone others choose to follow. Period! It is just that simple. A leader has followers. Despite title or position on an organizational chart, anyone on any level can be considered a leader in their organization or within a division. This is a very important concept to understand as you watch your team members develop and grow through the meaning-centered approach. As you see the "leaders," again, not by title, develop and emerge in your organization, you can capitalize on the opportunity to use these leaders as cheerleaders for the cause. This is also a great opportunity for you to build succession planning into your daily routine, preparing your natural leaders to become leaders by title as well.

You, too, may be developing your leadership pathway as you read this book. Remember that it is always necessary to develop yourself on a regular basis as a leader and an individual, personally and professionally. As technological advances continue to drive change in the workplace, it is important to constantly fine-tune leadership skills. You are urged to consider meaningful work as a fundamental human right and own your role in creating a meaningful space wherever your work takes you.

In the following chapters, we will discuss the 3Es of engagement, empowerment, and expertise. We will dive deeper into the essentials that make up each element of *Meaning-Centered Leadership*. Below are some graphics that outline the 3Es and the foundations that make up each of the elements. Leaders are in a position to influence others through the creation of meaning. We hope you will take up the challenge of becoming a *meaning-centered leader*, an agent for the transformative power of meaning.

The "How" with the 3 Es

Part I

ENGAGEMENT

People who find their lives meaningful usually have a goal that is challenging enough to take up all their energies, a goal that can add significance to their lives.

—Mihaly Csikszentmihalyi, *Flow*

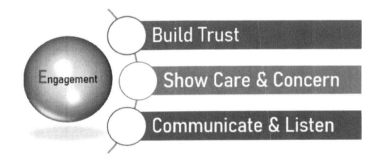

Elements of Engagement.

Before diving into the first element of *Meaning-Centered Leadership*, you will notice each part begins with a few reflection questions. Review and reflect upon each of these questions before moving into the actual content of the chapters. The overarching reflection questions discussed at the beginning of each element will provide some thoughtful and actionable ways to assess your leadership strategies.

Before beginning the chapter on engagement, think of the ways you currently engage your employees. Reflect on your current practices, and jot them down as you read. Do not spend a lot of time generating ideas; simply take a stream-of-consciousness approach and begin writing down anything that comes to mind. See how many strategies you are currently engaging with employees or colleagues in ways that lead to building trusting relationships. Again, do not overthink this process. Your answers should come quickly if you are currently spending time on these reflective actions. Do not spend more than five minutes on this exercise.

Reflection Questions for Engagement

Specific ways I engage with my employees include:

Specific ways I build trusting relationships include:

Specific ways I connect on a personal level with others include:

The ways I show others that I care about their well-being include:

Hopefully, you were able to generate a list that you can build on throughout this section. We will continue to provide reflection questions at the beginning of each element, as well as at the end of each chapter. Chances are you currently engage in some of the practices presented. In fact, most readers will intuitively understand the common sense of the *Meaning-Centered Leadership* approach, but unfortunately, as Tom Peters pointed out, very few leaders actually put these concepts into their daily practice.

It is our hope that at some point in time, you have used many of the techniques, strategies for success, and reflective practices that are outlined in this book. It is unlikely that you will have to overhaul your leadership practices completely; however, data point out that leaders need to focus on such practices consistently to build meaning. You will find many of these strategies common sense and you will likely innately realize these are simply the right things to do. The big question you must ask yourself is, *Am I doing this?*

Although leaders agree that these strategies are necessary to increase engagement, many let these strategies fall by the wayside when the days get busy and the work gets rough. It is imperative that leaders get back to the basics of what really matters—people! You are urged to think about refining your leadership so that *Meaning-Centered Leadership* is kept in the forefront of your practices. These practices cannot be touched just once or twice a year; they must be present in your daily behaviors.

Engagement is the first element in the *Meaning-Centered Leadership* approach. Time and time again, studies and research show that engagement is

at the forefront of successful organizations. This was outlined extensively in the first three chapters of this book; therefore, engagement is most certainly the first and the most important element of creating meaning in your organization.

High levels of engagement are essential to leadership effectiveness. In order to build deep engagement, you have to begin with the basic building blocks. Relationships built on trust are primary to building engagement, yet a relationship does not necessarily create engagement. A relationship can be superficial without going deep. An essential way for leaders to deepen their relationships is through open, honest, and authentic communication. Further, an engaged leader must have a high level of character while extolling virtues for the culture they hope to build. Leaders can build a valuable, meaningful culture when they establish open communication through active listening. These foundations of engagement—trust, care and concern, and open communication with active listening—are essential to *Meaning-Centered Leadership* practices.

The generation of workers you will lead in the future will demand engagement, and the generations you are currently leading desperately need it. According to the 2017 U.S. Census Bureau, the workforce consists of approximately 25 percent baby boomers (those born between 1946 and 1964), 33 percent Gen X (1965–1979), 35 percent millennials (1980–1994), and 5 percent Gen Z (1995–today) employees. With such a diverse set of employees in the workforce, it is necessary for leaders to understand the needs of each generation and how employees can be more engaged and happier in the workplace.

Recent reports of workforce engagement, as well as Gallup's 2019 book, *It's the Manager*, state that millennials and Gen Z employees do not just want a job for the paycheck; they instead want their work to matter. In fact, most millennials and Gen Z employees say they want their work to make a difference in the world. They want purpose in their work and they want to ensure that the work they do assimilates with their life.

Disengagement levels show that it is not just millennials and Gen Z employees seeking meaning and purpose. Most employees of today are craving meaning, regardless of the generation in which they were born. We are now hearing more on this topic as our Generation X and millennials are dominating the workforce, Gen Z are entering the workforce at rapid rates, and as baby boomers are getting ready to leave the workforce. Even the aging baby boomer population is now seeking self-actualization, the meaning in their life and in their work. Baby boomers are seeking to leave a lasting legacy and are striving to find purpose in what they do. Overall, employees are demanding meaning and purpose as all generations are realizing their importance. Referring back to Maslow's Hierarchy of Needs, people today are seeking that self-actualization, and it is here where meaning resides.

Research shows that today's workforce is craving a coach, not a manager. The true leaders of organizations going forward will play the role of coach. Autonomy will play a big part in an individual's workday. Back to the concept of *tell me what you want done and trust that I can find the pathway to achieve it.* Coaching requires ongoing conversations, not just an annual review. Coaching gives leadership the opportunity to help team members capitalize on their strengths. An organization should invest in continual professional development to teach their leaders the skills of coaching and assist them in how to lead with strength-based assessments.

In the next three chapters, as we discuss the first of the 3Es, engagement, you will see the overwhelming evidence that engagement is the primary key to organizational success. The element of engagement will be broken down as follows: chapter 4 will cover the element of trust as it relates to engagement, chapter 5 will discuss care and concern, and chapter 6 will cover open communication with active listening.

It is imperative to advance relationships built on trust, care and concern, and open communication with active listening. These foundational elements of engagement need to be the initial areas of focus in becoming an exemplary leader. By focusing on the behaviors and strategies suggested, you will develop the relationships necessary to have a deeply engaged workforce. As you have seen in the previous chapters, engagement is critical. Without changing the paradigm of the employees who are actively disengaged, your organization will not sustain.

Again, to assist you in this journey, each chapter has resources and reflections. We urge you to pace your progress. Really, think deeply about each element of the 3Es. Create opportunities to establish that you have a message that is worthy of your followers' attention. You will take the first step in becoming a meaning-centered leader. Put down the book. Practice. Reflect. Make notes as you go through your workday on how you currently handle each element and how you can improve upon each element by utilizing the strategies, tips, and techniques provided.

It is also vitally important as a leader to create more leaders. Be sure to pay attention to the behaviors and strategies of others. Remember, a "leader" is not a leader by title; a leader is a leader based on the fact that others follow. Find the leaders in your organizational workgroups—even if they don't have the job by title. Watch them. See how they engage. See how they handle the elements. Reflect and refine. Give yourself the time to think deeply about your practice and the practices of those around you. Plan appropriate adjustments that will build upon your strengths and maximize your impact. Let's get started!

Chapter 4

Trust

You can't have success without trust.

—Jim Burke, Former Chairman
and CEO, Johnson & Johnson

During a recent appearance in Lake Worth, Florida, leadership guru John C. Maxwell suggested that the people you lead are interested in the following three questions: *Do you care for me? Can you help me? Can I trust you?* Relationships built on trust must be a top priority in your organization. Throughout the research, the followers surveyed described trust as the most important element of their leader's character. Respondents reacted most strongly to the question that asked them about the importance of their leaders' ability to establish trust among their team and throughout the organization. Trust was also a central theme when the leaders were asked what they do to develop relationships within the organization. One leader explained that trusting relationships create a healthy environment, while another offered that true relationships come from trust.

Throughout the various industries that the meaning-making research was carried out, one consistent finding was that followers rank character highest among those leadership elements thought to bring meaning. A closer look at the research reveals that the survey respondents identified that the leader must demonstrate character with behaviors that show they can be trusted and they must behave in a manner that is ethical. In one of the studies 100 percent of the respondents rated these two areas, trust and character, as critically important.

The exemplary leaders often expressed the same urgency about character and issues related to building trust. The exemplary leaders expressed an urgency with regard to building trust. It is evident that both leaders and followers are aware of the essential need for trust to be present.

The voices of these exemplary leaders often echoed a very similar refrain. The notion of following a strong moral compass and solid values was ever present in these interviews. There was quite often agreement that it is the small day-to-day things that leaders do that lead to trust building. They expressed the need to have a value system that guides the daily activities and that the leaders need to hold themselves accountable.

It is perhaps no surprise that character resonated with both the leaders and the followers in this research. The operational definition of character is alignment with a value system that promotes ethical thoughts and actions based on principles of concern for others through optimism and integrity while being reliable, transparent, and authentic. When you look at that definition, you can see the essential elements of trust building. We trust someone who expresses concern toward us in ways that demonstrate they are authentic, reliable, and optimistic.

From this foundation of strong character, which leads to trust building, both the exemplary leaders and the followers mentioned the need for strong relationships. The undeniable link between trust and relationship building is evident here. The exemplary leaders described the need to let their followers know they care about them. They described structuring activities that allowed them to get to know their colleagues while simultaneously creating opportunities for relationships throughout the organization to develop and grow. This relationship building presents an opportunity for trust to grow. More importantly, these trusting relationships are foundational to the creation of meaning.

The findings are supported by a plethora of research and writing that are devoted to trust. In the *Speed of Trust: The One Thing That Changes Everything*, Covey and Merrill described trust as the key leadership competency of the new global economy. Trust is truly the foundation for all other forms of engagement and must exist for a relationship to not only survive but thrive! Covey and Merrill further explained: "Contrary to what most people believe, trust is not some soft, illusive quality that you either have or you don't; rather, trust is a pragmatic, tangible actionable asset that you can create much faster than you probably think possible."[1] They also offer that trust means confidence, and the opposite of trust is suspicion. If you think about people that you trust, this definition makes sense. You do not question the motives of a trustworthy person, nor do you wonder what their end game might be. You know you can count on them. You know you can trust them!

Trust's definition is purposeful, straightforward, and reflected by numerous leadership experts. Trust should be at the forefront of the leader's mind. Trust starts with telling the truth and being consistent in deed and action.

Trust is knowing that one will do what they say they are going to do, and it is grounded in integrity and honesty. Trust, therefore, can be defined as having confidence and faith in someone.

Leaders Eat Last, by Simon Sinek, illustrated that leaders must create a circle of safety anchored by trust. He describes his takeaways from spending time with the U.S. Marines, where he discusses his learnings in leadership. He said the Marines understand that leadership is about integrity, honesty, and accountability, all components of trust. Sinek had a few definitions of his own. He voiced that a true leader tells the truth. Integrity and trust are part of the same equation.

With this solid definition of trust in mind, we can begin to look at the role of trust in building relationships that will help you and your followers experience workplace meaning. Without trust, relationships cannot be formed. Think back to your various jobs. Have you ever had a leader, or even a colleague, you did not trust? Have you ever had a leader who made empty promises? What about follow-through? Have you experienced a leader who has said they will get back to you, but then they never did? All of these examples are grounded in trust, or lack thereof. Many of these examples may seem trivial if they stand alone, but each and every time a situation like this takes place, trust erodes. As trust erodes, so does the confidence of the followers. Eventually, as these small infractions occur, team members will lose the trust and faith they have in the leader. The downward spiral of trust erosion can be detrimental to the overall performance of a team.

The authors of *Becoming a Resonant Leader*, McKee, Boyatzis, and Johnston, described the ability to inspire trust as one of the keys to great leadership. Trust is the first, and perhaps the greatest, link in developing the relationships that are needed for building meaning. Authors Dave and Wendy Ulrich concur. In their book *The Why of Work*, they explained that passionate teams are created by leaders who have built trusting relationships. Building such trusting relationships leads to a work environment of which people want to be a part. Trusting relationships, not only between leaders and followers but among all team members, will lead to an overall better workplace. The existence of good work relationships, created by effective leaders, leads to good business and allows for the mediation of problems. High-performing teams are marked by mentoring relationships, friendships, and positive networks: teams that can solve complex problems and adapt to change. The role of the leader is to help followers have positive work relationships that will allow for feelings of abundance and meaning to be increased.

The modern workplace also calls for rapid innovation and change. Trust is a vital necessity for creating an environment where others can take risks and explore innovative responses to problems they and the company are facing. The exemplary leaders interviewed in our research expressed that trust is a necessary precursor to establishing healthy relationships and a healthy environment. Trusting relationships help to create an environment where people can take risks, an essential element of an innovative workforce. One exemplary leader who was interviewed stated that without trusting relationships, there would be a fear of failure. Nearly every leader interviewed cited that developing relationships built on the foundation of trust is an important component of their leadership strategies.

The necessity of building trusting relationships was not only found in our research with exemplary leaders but has been substantiated throughout the literature on impactful leadership theories. Transformational leadership suggested that fully developing all people in the organization is the goal and also that the followers in the organization should operate knowing that is the goal. The theory suggested that creating an environment that fosters creativity and promotes risk-taking could be accomplished if the leaders took responsibility for their followers.

Individual consideration is a component of transformational leadership that suggests each leader is responsible for building trusting relationships that contribute toward follower and organizational transformation. Similarly, authentic leadership was described as a way that leaders could assist people in finding connection and meaning through the building of transparent relationships and decision making.

An ethical climate will build commitment and trust among followers. By including team members in the development of relationships built on trust, we are offered insight into the growing knowledge that by focusing on follower relationships and creating a trusting and caring environment, the impact of your leadership can be amplified.

Moreover, Gallup research found that employees in high-trust organizations report that they are twice as likely to be with their organizations in a year. On the contrary, employees in low-trust organizations are busy looking for their next job. As discussed in previous chapters, employee turnover is quite costly to an organization. Employees who are considering leaving the company are not listening to new directives or participating in change initiatives because they have already made the decision to leave the company. In the meantime, they are a drag on productivity and will likely add to the toxicity of the workplace. Trust erodes between leader and the soon-to-be departing employee. The damage caused by lack of trust does not end when mistrusting employees leave the organization. Through their networks, they continue to broadcast that the organization lacks trust. This can potentially repel other job candidates and hamper recruitment efforts.

The research on the impact of trust leads us to the next logical step as leaders. We must build trust. We offer the following three overarching ideas for focusing on the development of trust within your organization. These ideas on building trust should sound very familiar, as they are rooted in universal truths of human behavior.

Before going on, we urge you to identify how your current work connects to your larger sense of purpose. What is your "Why"? Whether you put God at the center, as Rick Warren suggests in *The Purpose Driven Life*, or you follow another spiritual path, or none at all, it is imperative that your work connects to your larger sense of purpose. As Richard J. Leider discusses in his 2015 book *The Power of Purpose: Find Meaning, Live Longer, Better*, find a purpose that puts your goal outside of your norm, something that is larger than yourself, one that creates overall meaning in your life and the lives of others.

One way to gain clarity with regard to your purpose is to write a succinct personal vision statement. We will go more into detail on your personal vision statement in chapter 13, but to begin the discussion, your personal vision statement should embody what excites you, what motivates you to continue to do the work you do, and what inspires you to make a difference in the world. Your personal vision statement should set apart your dreams and vision for the future. If your work then connects to that vision statement in tangible ways, you will be able to work purposefully each and every day. Your believability as a leader will grow exponentially if you are leading from a deep sense of purpose.

First, you must define your truth with regard to your work and the people you serve. As a leader, it is imperative that your work is filled with great purpose. Motivation and energy flow from purpose. If you are deeply connected to your work, others will see it and will be inspired to follow your lead. You will build a foundation for trust to develop because you approach your work in an optimal state. You must also trust the people you serve. If you approach others with pessimism and distrust, you will construct a culture that replicates pessimism and lack of trust.

For example, Ed's personal mission statement is, "To improve society through education." As an educator in an administrative leadership position, Ed is able to work toward that end with purpose each and every day. That purpose has sustained him through more than thirty years of work. More importantly, developing a purposeful and clear vision statement has allowed him to work truthfully toward personal goals, truthful to himself, and truthful to those he serves as a leader.

Second, you must also trust the people you serve. One way to develop trust is to first extend trust. Think of a situation that will allow you to extend trust to others in your organization. By respectfully trusting others, you build their optimism and increase the likelihood that trust will grow in your organization.

Third, you must understand that trust is a road built slowly, but it can most certainly be destroyed instantly. Building trusting relationships is a matter of making and keeping commitments. To connect with others, you need to find areas of mutual interest and make commitments over and over again. Trust building needs to be an intentional and focused practice that you never stop developing. You must guard against trust busters. When you fail to deliver on promises or commitments, both big and small, show ill will due to temper tantrums, or show undue favoritism, you can erode trust. You must also guard against unintentional acts that destroy organizational trust.

Consider the following true story of organizational trust breaking. In this situation, a director promised the team members $10 Starbuck's cards for completing an online training module. Since this was a new adventure, the team was pumped up. All the team members completed the modules. Days passed. No cards. A couple of weeks passed. No cards. The team members waited in anticipation for their reward. The calls and texts started among the employees: "Did you get your Starbuck's card?" The cards, unfortunately, never came.

Sadly, the story does not end there. During a face-to-face meeting months later, someone brought up the fact that the cards never came. The director casually said, "Oh no! We will get those sent out." But again, the cards never came. After another few months, it became an inside joke among the sales team, "Hey where are the Starbuck's cards?" The damage was done. Trust continued to erode.

When the next training module was set to be taken, very few people participated, and eventually, those modules stopped. Furthermore, when the next competition was announced, and the reward was a jacket, one employee mockingly texted the others saying, "My Starbuck's card better be in the pocket of that jacket!" Empty promises, though seemingly trivial, became the brunt of jokes and depleted trust within the division.

It is doubtful that the director set out to erode trust with others in the organization or to damage the company's reputation with its employees, but that is exactly what happened. Furthermore, the sales team members made comments about the leadership just not caring. It had virtually nothing to do with the minor Starbuck's reward and more to do with caring about the team and following through on the promises made, no matter how big or small.

Unintentionally breaking trust and breaking promises can have dire consequences within an organization. It is critical to follow-through on your promises with employees and customers alike. Examples like the Starbuck's cards are constant in organizations. Surely you have seen similar small acts or oversights turn into bigger problems. Trust can be built up quite easily with follow-through of seemingly simple or trivial promises, but remember it can crumble down even faster if follow-through does not happen. Just as a parent says to their child, do not make promises you cannot keep. This simple fact of keeping promises, big and small, affects any type of relationship in any setting.

The impact of your leadership is directly tied to how much others trust you. Trust will serve to deepen your connections with others and allow your relationships to flourish. The trust you develop will strengthen commitment and effort. Perhaps most importantly, trust is needed to help develop an atmosphere where organizational meaning can be created.

And remember, the exact opposite holds true for the above statements. Your leadership can take a complete turn for the worse without trust. Lack of trust can completely diminish and deplete connections with your team members, so much so that instead of flourishing, the connections die quite rapidly. Finally, lack of trust leads to lack of meaning. As noted by numerous leaders and authors, trust is the glue that can hold a team together. Without trust, the pieces will surely peel away and eventually fall by the wayside.

According to Patrick Lencioni, author of *The Five Dysfunctions of a Team: A Leadership Fable*, a leader must demonstrate vulnerability to encourage teams to build trust. Genuine displays of vulnerability by the leader can help create an environment where vulnerability is not punished. *Genuine* is the key word! Employees can see when someone is not genuine in their display of vulnerability. Others can tell if the vulnerability is coming from a place like a box to be checked because a coach told them to do it or a book said it is important to be vulnerable.

When team members can be truly vulnerable, they are more likely to share ideas and ask for help. By showing their human side, a leader can develop rapport with the team. Without vulnerability, trust will not grow and neither will the meaning in your organization. Fortunately, there are several steps you can take to build organizational trust and you can role model your own vulnerability in the process.

Internal organizational trust is only half of the puzzle to success, though. Not only do those inside the organization need to have trust but so do the external stakeholders. Consumers want to trust that the products or services offered by an organization will do what they say it will do. Consumers must trust that their personal information will remain safe and secure. Consumers must trust that the organization is staying true to their vision, mission, and values. Research has shown that consumer spending correlates to the trust that they have in the organization. If trust is low, spending will be low.

Organizations must ensure that all stakeholders, including all employees and the customers, experience trust. To maintain trust with both internal and external stakeholders, a leader has to see the customers' perception of the organization from the standpoint of trust. How an organization collects, manages, and uses customer data should be clear and transparent to all stakeholders.

In summary, trust is a key component of increasing employee engagement and satisfaction. Below are some strategies for success to build a trusting environment within your organization. But remember, these practices must be authentic and practiced often to be effective in building a meaning-centered culture.

STRATEGIES FOR SUCCESS

Throughout the following chapters, as we define the three elements of *Meaning-Centered Leadership*, we will provide strategies for success. Again, research has shown that, though these strategies seem simple and logical, very few leaders are consistently implementing them. Like a January New Year's resolution diet plan, strategies like those you see listed below are implemented only short-term and then they fall by the wayside. Consistent implementation of these strategies will help you lead with increased meaning in your organization. Consistency is key! It is critical that all leaders implement and consistently practice the strategies that build stronger connections built on the foundations of trust. Below we will discuss the steps to building trust in your organizations with some strategies you can implement today.

Positive Interpersonal Relationships

One key to building trust in an organization is to build strong interpersonal connections. Leaders must create opportunities for followers to build bonds and establish positive patterns of interaction. The first three strategies in this section address that need. The return on investment for the time spent building the relationships within your organization will pay you back over and over again.

One way to build interpersonal relationships is to provide employees the opportunity to talk. Employees must be able to converse openly, with each other and with the leadership. Research has shown that setting up environments for spontaneous conversations to take place can pay dividends back to the organization. Think back to the "water cooler conversations," but on a whole new level.

One office that Barbara worked with had a beautiful lounge for employees to relax in during breaks or even if they needed to just get up and away from their desk. This area simply had comfortable couches and lounge chairs, small tables, and calming photos on the walls. The lounge became the meeting spot for all to just hang out and chat. Oftentimes ad hoc meetings would form in this comfortable space and some great conversations and ideas would surface, but more importantly, this space gave the team members a place to let down their guard and just share about life in general.

It is in such open and inviting spaces that interpersonal relationships are formed. It is here where each employee can learn about others on a personal level: *Who has children? Who is married? Who has ill parents? Who just had a baby or got a new puppy? Who is up? Who is down? Who needs a hug? And who is celebrating an important event?* It is here where meaningful relationships and conversations take place. It is here where meaning is formed!

Meeting Icebreakers

Team meetings are an excellent opportunity to build trust with your teams. A small amount of time should be spent in trust-building activities at the beginning of all team meetings, be they face-to-face or virtual, and should occur first on the meeting agenda.

Allowing time for simple meeting icebreakers can be hugely rewarding for team members. Icebreakers can create opportunities to deepen connections, encourage vulnerability, and build bonds between team members. Meetings that take time to build trust between team members will strengthen your organization and your ability to lead a high-functioning team. There are numerous engaging short icebreakers that you can find that will not dig into too much of your precious meeting time but are assured to build trust and enthusiasm among your team members. Some examples include:

1. State your name, position, and your favorite ice cream.
2. State your favorite fall (spring, summer, winter) activity.
3. Announce one thing others in the room may not know about you.
4. Pick a number off a list of random questions and answer the question.
5. Share a time that you were most inspired by someone or something.
6. What was your favorite part of your childhood and why?
7. If you could travel to a new country every year, which country would you visit first, second, and third?

Icebreaker activities such as these are short and easy but are effective in creating better relationships and enthusiasm among team members. These can be used both virtually and in face-to-face meetings. You will find that the first few times you add an icebreaker, the smiles form and the enthusiasm goes up so much that it may be difficult to reel the team back in. Be sure to plan a little extra time the first few times. As you add an icebreaker to every agenda, reeling in the team members will get easier over time. The icebreaker will become a part of what they do and will also aid in sparking conversations to build interpersonal relationships outside the meeting as team members get to know each other on a deeper level.

Whip Arounds

Another way to build trust among teams in team meetings is to create opportunities for praise. By simply structuring opportunities for colleagues to acknowledge one another's efforts, you can build trust. Structured opportunities must also be augmented with spontaneous opportunities. For example, starting meetings with a quick whip around that allows each member to acknowledge another team member can dramatically escalate the positive feelings in the meeting room. These opportunities for praise take only a few minutes, and they serve to deepen connections and build meaning. Encourage spontaneity and authenticity in these whip arounds.

Team-Building Activities

Team-building activities are another great way to build trust. Engage with your teams in fun activities, both on-site and off-site. When team members take time to celebrate, they get the opportunity to get to know one another outside of the office. This allows them to see each other as human beings. Taking time to plan and implement team-building activities can deepen the connections your employees need to develop meaning. Some simple examples include potluck lunches for holidays, monthly luncheons to celebrate the birthdays in that month, scavenger hunts, decorating contests, and so on. These small acts of engagement may cost a bit of time and money, but your organization will reap the rewards through increased engagement and trust.

One president spoke of how his weekly leadership team meetings take place on a trail behind the college. The team goes for a walk in the fresh air and they discuss items of the week. By being in nature and exercising at the same time, the team is more relaxed and engaged. He stated that these Monday meetings are more thought-provoking and problem-solving than all other meetings in the board room. There is something special about getting out of the office and into nature that brings out the best in people.

Two important reminders when creating on-site and off-site activities: First, if you work in a dispersed model, ensure that the budget allows for these activities to be replicated, preferably the same day, throughout the system. Trust, team spirit, and enthusiasm will all be diminished if the corporate headquarters seems to be favored over other locations. This is especially true in today's highly visible world through postings on social media. Be sure that all team members are thanked and recognized in a similar fashion.

Second, be cognizant of having alcohol at work functions. This is often a common practice, but in today's society, it can be a mixture for trouble! First, not everyone partakes in alcohol consumption and they may not feel comfortable attending. Further, it is especially important that leadership not partake in excessive alcohol intake as judgment becomes impaired and guards may fall down. Alcohol can erode character and integrity and can be personality altering. If alcohol is part of the festivities, ensure that drinks are limited to just one or two as there are many liabilities involved in providing alcohol at a work function. This is a cautionary measure, but oftentimes many choose to ignore this very important warning. We have all witnessed all too often the effects of alcohol and the irreparable damage it can cause.

DEMONSTRATING TRUSTWORTHINESS

Trustworthiness is a multifaceted construct. Research shows that leaders who are perceived to have high ability, a firm moral compass, and compassion for their followers are perceived as trustworthy. It is essential that your followers are able to trust that your deeds and actions are consistent and in line with the core values you espouse. Further, it is important that your actions demonstrate a high degree of personal competence and that you treat others fairly, equally, and with compassion.

Without trustworthiness your leadership efforts will cause disengagement and lead to increased turnover. If your moods swing wildly and others are not sure how or when to approach you, your impact will be diminished. Similarly, if you are naturally introverted and/or possessed of a brooding personality, others will not seek you out. The reflection questions at the end of this section provide you with several excellent opportunities to examine the ways that you demonstrate trustworthiness.

Emotional Regulation

One intentional effort you should make every day is to be the calm in the storm for others in your organization. This starts with being consistent in your emotional response to all issues that impact your organization. Emotional intelligence, and the ability to regulate your emotions, is a very important trait for an exemplary leader. In fact, the book titled *Emotional Intelligence 2.0*, by Travis Bradberry and Jean Greaves, is a great place to start if you want to learn more about this great practice.

A leader who is ranting and raving cannot serve their organization well and does not demonstrate emotional intelligence. People in your organization need to trust that, even in crisis situations, you will respond in ways that restore order and assist in returning stability.

Emotional deregulation can hyperinflate issues and create unnecessary stress within an organization. There is a time and place for tension, but it must be managed effectively or you risk destabilizing your organization. We will come back to emotional regulation later in the book, when we look at the role of emotional intelligence. The fact that you find that term throughout the book should be a clear statement of its importance to your leadership.

Value Adds

We all have a series of work-related tasks to complete each and every day. If you approach those tasks with an eye on adding value throughout your organization, your abilities will be displayed for others to see. Furthermore, you will have the opportunity to engage with others in the completion of their tasks. As others perceive your ability to create better outcomes, you will deepen their engagement and ensure you are viewed as a trustworthy leader.

The Moral Compass

A leader's actions are always under scrutiny by their followers. Therefore, it is the leader's responsibility and moral obligation to ensure the values and ethics of an organization are upheld. For example, if you witness employee behavior that violates agreed-upon norms or procedures, do you immediately call it out? If you witness questionable behaviors, words, or actions, such as racial slurs or sexual connotations, do you have the strength to report it? It is imperative that a leader take action when witnessing such offenses.

Establishing guidelines and then not enforcing these behaviors or not addressing value violations creates a morally ambiguous environment. If you do not report witnessed concern immediately, your team's trust in you will surely erode. A strong moral compass ensures employees that the rules of engagement are understood and embraced by all. Leaders who are strong in supporting universal moral principles, such as do no harm or treat others the way you expect to be treated, create higher engagement and, as a result, experience less employee turnover.

In the table titled Reflection Questions for Trust, you will find some questions that you can ponder to assess your own personal level of trust. Further, you can have conversations with team members about how they would answer these questions, not only about you but also about themselves. Take a few minutes to reflect upon your leadership style by answering the questions thoughtfully.

My succinct personal mission statement that clarifies my purpose is:

Specific ways I extend trust to others include:

Intentional efforts I take to build trust on a day-to-day basis include:

Opportunities I provide for colleagues to acknowledge one another's efforts include:

Celebrations I have planned for my team include:

Chapter 5

Care and Concern

Demonstrating care—giving heart to people in the broadest sense—is essential to maximizing human potential and achievement.

—Mark C. Crowley, *Lead from the Heart*

Trust is essential, and one of the first things a meaning-centered leader can do to build trust is to demonstrate care and concern. Through the years, numerous authors have discussed the need for leaders to demonstrate care and concern. In fact, in life itself, human beings express the overall need to be wanted and cared for. As discussed previously, dating back to the 1940s with research from Abraham Maslow and the human motivation theory, Maslow states that the physiological and safety needs must be met before progressing to higher needs, including belongingness and love. These needs lead us all to the pathway of self-actualization and meaning.

Care and concern help to fulfill the needs of the pyramid on the road to self-actualization and meaning. Why should it be any different in the workplace? As Stephen Covey and Tom Peters have suggested throughout their decades of teaching about leadership, the basics of *just being a good human being* transcend into the workplace. Caring about others, and showing concern for them, is vital to developing engagement and relationships with your colleagues. It is all so simple, yet seems to be ignored when in the work environment.

What might care and concern look like in the workplace? It can be as simple as greeting everyone you pass in the hallway and writing notes of appreciation for a job well done. It can be just listening to others as they share about their weekend. Simple, yet so elusive. Consider scenarios like this:

Have you ever walked into an organization and no one looks up when you pass by? Have you ever walked through your own hallway and just passed by others, without eye contact, without a hello? These situations are all too common in the workplace, and this lack of concern for others depletes an organization's culture. In fact, in one simple experiment we tested just this. In passing eighty-seven people in one day, without our saying a word of prompting, only four people initiated a verbal hello. Four!

Now consider this instead: walk down the hallway with a smile on your face, your head held high, and greeting everyone you meet with an encouraging *hello* or *good morning.* Watch how this simple gesture can make others smile and put a pep in their step for the day. In testing this scenario, the numbers nearly reversed. People responded with a hello right back! Amazing what one simple word can do to change a culture and give a feeling of belongingness, a feeling of love.

In his book *Make It Matter*, Scott Mautz described the meaning-making process as one in which leaders build teams that authentically care for one another. Mautz added that a caring, connective undercurrent is established when leaders show respect and demonstrate genuine care for others.

Similarly, Mark C. Crowley, author of *Lead from the Heart*, cited similar research that expressed the need for creating a meaningful environment. The participants in the research expressed that the absence of concern, care, and connection from their leaders was a primary reason for the discontent that employees experience. Workers really want to be cared for individually, on a personal level, even within the workplace.

In our research, the twelve coresearchers developed a definition of character that included how a leader expresses a value system that promotes ethical thoughts and actions based on principles of care and concern for others through optimism and integrity while being reliable, transparent, and authentic.

When surveyed about the importance of how leaders build relationships within their organizations, the followers in our research declared that the leader must behave in ways that show they care about team members. From the perspective of the followers in our research, demonstrating care and concern is an essential prerequisite for building relationships. It is an essential step in the process of developing trusting relationships. Followers need to see that the leader acts in ways that consistently show they care about the well-being of all members of the organization.

Across the industries studied in the meaning research, essential agreement was found. Whether they were university presidents, CEOs, or chiefs of police, the leaders all mentioned the importance of the human connection by demonstrating that they care. These exemplary leaders went on to explain the importance of being available and having an open-door policy. They stated they need to be visible and interact with everyone. And during those interactions, they need to treat everyone with dignity and respect.

Throughout the research, the common theme of being visible throughout the organization and communicating the importance of others' work was described by the exemplary leaders. This important step was connected to the leaders' statements that they believed their people need to know that the leadership of the organization cared about each member. The leaders described the need to take an interest in their followers. Several of the exemplary leaders expressed this as a process of being around their followers and ensuring that their needs are being met.

The exemplary leaders' expressions of the need to communicate trust, and build relationships by taking an active role in the process of showing followers that they care, were echoed by the followers in their survey responses. Strong agreement was found among the followers that a leader needs to continuously promote team unity while behaving in a way that shows they care about all team members.

The exemplary leaders and their followers were clear: demonstrating care and concern is an essential element of their work experience. As such, it is one of the ways that leaders can begin to develop the resonant relationships that can be a bridge to creating meaning in their organizations. Balancing expressions of care and concern throughout the milieu of a busy day can be a challenge; however, a focus on care and concern is essential even when having difficult conversations and managing problematic issues.

Care and concern opportunities create meaning for both the leader and the follower. The creation of meaning is a two-way street and everyone benefits. When a leader expresses care and concern in a true and authentic fashion, all parties benefit. As leaders express their care toward others, leaders reported that they, too, become happier and more content in their positions as leaders. Leaders said it "just makes them feel good" when they dive deeper on a human level with their team members.

When facing adversity or challenging times, it is even more critical for a leader to demonstrate concern. A leader is faced with the compelling need to simultaneously support a fallen team member and ensure a replacement with adequate training can continue to do the job. Seeing to that both of those important positions are attended to is essential to demonstrating a caring approach to all team members. The organization is watching during these moments to determine whether or not the leader is truly demonstrating care and concern for their colleagues. Attending to both tasks with equal focus is essential to being a caring leader.

Other researchers have drawn the same conclusions about the need for leaders to demonstrate care and concern. Social determination theorist researchers have concluded that employees experience a deeper sense of belonging, stronger emotional attachment, and stronger affiliation when the leader exhibits concern for the health and well-being of employees. These theorists also concluded that the deeper emotional attachment experienced as a result of a caring approach helps followers develop deeper intrinsic motivation, allowing for a stronger internalization of organizational goals.

Creating a caring organization should be the leader's goal. Beyond the individual acts of caring that we mention in this chapter, in the preceding chapters we discuss the importance of collaboration. Researchers have found that collaborative practices, such as shared leadership, help to build organizational caring. As a leader demonstrates caring for their followers, they must also focus on building a culture where caring is part of the culture. The collaborative practices highlighted in the upcoming chapters should be seen as part of the leader's mandate for building a caring organizational culture.

For care to be seen as part of the company culture, the leader must take steps to be a caring individual and an unrelenting boss when this cultural norm is violated. Holding others accountable to an expectation of caring behavior is essential. Understanding the importance of creating a workplace with strong caring relationships that lead to meaning-making is requisite. As the caring relationships in your organization multiply, your employees will demonstrate deeper attachment and will be much more likely to stay engaged. Those same employees may also become your best recruiting tool. Having a cadre of supporters who share with others the positive feelings they associate with your organization will drive other high-quality job seekers your way. This will become more critical and commonplace as even higher numbers of millennials and Gen Z employees enter the workforce.

Showing concern for others is an expression of a leader's character. A healthy organization pursues its goals with an eye on balancing organizational needs in a way that benefits everyone. Leadership that pursues strong organizational outcomes with an equal eye on the well-being of everyone within the organization creates valuable opportunities to promote well-being while pursuing profitability. Consider again how the top 181 CEOs of the Business Roundtable have made exactly this concept part of the new vision for all organizations. This information will continue to resonate among the cream of the crop in successful organizations. When a company cares about their people, the organization will thrive!

Demonstrating care and concern allows your leadership impact to deepen. When others can affirmatively answer the question asked in chapter 4, *Do you care for me?*, they are better able to experience corrective feedback that supports their professional development. When you look at the strategies for success in this area, you will see they are essentially opportunities for you to have authentic interactions with your employees. It is within these authentic conversational opportunities that your direct impact can be magnified. When others know that you are interested in their well-being, as well as the organization's well-being, they are better able to see the two as mutually inclusive.

STRATEGIES FOR SUCCESS

Below you will find easy-to-implement strategies for showing care and concern. Implementation of strategies such as these will help you lead with increased meaning. Again, it is critical that you become consistent and regular in the use of these strategies to ensure team members know you are serious about implementation. The strategies outlined below—open-door policy, care through coaching, and handwritten notes of appreciation—are just a few simple ways to show you care. Research shows the power of care and concern is foundational to building true and authentic relationships. By building care and concern, you will increase engagement, happiness, and meaning. Out of all the strategies for success, this is one of the most important strategies to build, yet one of the most overlooked because it is considered soft. Do not overlook this important concept! In fact, give this some great attention at the outset and watch your team transform.

Open-Door Policy

Recall a leader who demonstrated caring for you as an individual and ask yourself, *How did that caring make me feel?* More importantly, think back to how that leader's ability to demonstrate caring impacted not only you but also the team and the organization as a whole.

One simple tool to implement for demonstrating care and concern is a true open-door policy. That is, ensure that your team, regardless of position, knows that your door, and every door of every leader in your organization, is always open to listen to compliments, concerns, new ideas, or even just small talk. Warning! If you declare an open-door policy, but then you do not follow through, it can be devastating to the team and to the trust you have built with team members. Do not state you will have an open-door policy if you are going to dismiss or negate any comment, question, or concern that comes your way. Being dismissive when making the promise of an open-door policy can break trust faster than your heart can beat. Be ready to actually follow through on your open-door policy if someone chooses to pass through it!

An example of an effective open-door policy comes from Ed's early years of teaching. Early in his teaching career, Ed worked for a principal, Craig Rydquist. Principal Rydquist, now Associate Superintendent Rydquist, had an open-door policy. Any time you wanted to drop in for a discussion, it was okay. Ed frequently took advantage of his open-door policy to get his perspective. He always came away feeling validated and informed. That small gesture of time was invaluable in Ed's development as a leader and teacher. Those and other expressions of caring were felt by all the staff and faculty. In the thirty years of public and private service in education, Ed has seldom worked with a more harmonious team than during those early years when La Loma Junior High School was led by Principal Rydquist.

Beyond this anecdotal experience, the research is clear that there are many benefits to an open-door policy. First and foremost, this policy ensures open and ongoing dialogue. Open dialogue can help lead to constant organizational improvement as questions are answered in a timely fashion. Also, employee morale will be positively impacted by the opportunity for their leader to demonstrate that they care about employee issues. Finally, an open-door policy brings issues to light that might otherwise remain dormant until they explode in an eruption of expensive litigation. When employees are able to be heard, they give the leader an opportunity to respond to issues that might erode the culture or, even worse, lead to lawsuits and damages to the other workers.

Care through Coaching

Demonstrating care and concern means understanding one's goals and aspirations, even if your team members are not quite sure of the direction at the time. A great leader becomes a coach—one who digs deeply and regularly with their team members. It is important to ask questions about a person's goals and aspirations. Help guide your employees to a greater goal.

The best of leaders create more leaders through coaching and conversation. By asking simple questions like: *Where do you want to be in two years, five years, ten years? What is the best part of your job that truly inspires you and gives you meaning? What is your least favorite part of your job, and why?* These probing questions show that you are concerned about their future and their career growth.

To bring this example to life, let's talk about two different leaders: one who lacks care and concern for others, and another who deeply exemplifies a coach and mentor. When Ed was still a teenager and serving in a Marine Corps infantry platoon, the first platoon commander he served under, we'll call him Lieutenant T (for Texas), struggled to lead the platoon and clearly demonstrates a story of someone who lacks the ability to show care and concern. We were a hardscrabble lot from all corners of the United States. Ed's platoon brothers were bull riders from Oklahoma, poor boys from Guam, inner-city boys from rust-belt cities in decay, and a host of lost boys from cities as far apart as Seattle and Brooklyn. All platoon members shared a common uniform and training, but in the barracks, they were a divided and quarrelsome band of renegades. Lieutenant T's leadership did nothing to change that. His leadership style seemed to increase the mistrust and acrimony that was ever present in the air. The dysfunction as a unit became apparent when in the field on training exercises. Lieutenant T's inability to communicate caused injury and nearly death to several young men. The final straw was his misguidance of explosive ordnance that almost killed the combined command of the company and the leaders of a South Korean Marine training group.

And now let's see the opposite. Let's discuss a commanding officer who demonstrated true care and concern. This leader was observant and made one life-changing comment that would change the trajectory of Ed's life. The story continued when Ed came back state-side and the team found themselves with a new platoon commander, Lieutenant O (for Ohio). Lieutenant O had a great knack for showing care and concern, and it made a world of difference, both to Ed personally and to the platoon. The first thing Lieutenant O did was call each and every member of the platoon to his office for a formal meeting. In military style, all soldiers marched to the front of his desk, came to attention, and shouted, "Reporting as ordered Sir." After giving the command, "At ease," Lieutenant O spoke with each platoon member while looking through the service records. He told Ed, "I can see by your test scores you're too intelligent not to be educated." He handed him a schedule of classes and said, "Here is your class schedule; you are going to night school to earn your high school diploma." During one of those night classes, an instructor called Ed to the front of the class and demanded to know how he was getting 100 percent on all his tests. Let's just say previous high school experiences did not include a lot of positive contact with teachers and other authority figures, so Ed was apprehensive. The instructor said, "Nobody aces my tests; you're really smart. If you do not reenlist, you should go to college." Ed's apprehension was immediately replaced with a moment of clarity that changed his life. Ed left that class with a new mantra: "I'm really smart and I'm going to college, yes me!" From the foster care system to a homeless high school dropout, Ed was now a man with a plan: "I'm going to college!" But this story isn't about how Lieutenant O's leadership impacted only Ed's life, although he will never forget him for leading him to his future education; this story is about how Lieutenant O's leadership impacted the lost boys of weapons company.

Ed can't be certain how Lieutenant O's conversations went with all of the other platoon brothers, but he does know how the platoon changed. Lieutenant O set an example of caring and positive interactions with the platoon members. Where Lieutenant T was cold, diffident, and dismissive, Lieutenant O was warm and engaging. He gave all the caring like that of a big brother, which all platoon members needed. He stepped in if someone stepped out of line, but he was full of positive energy in his leadership. The barracks became a friendlier place. When the platoon ran down the parade deck at the end of a physical training session, they thundered loud and proud.

One leader can have a profound impact. Especially a leader who is willing to build engagement by investing in creating an atmosphere where trusting relationships can flourish. Lieutenant O cared and the platoon thrived.

Handwritten Notes of Appreciation

Simple and practical practices of showing care and concern have been woven throughout leadership books. We challenge you to consider how these seemingly small acts of kindness can make a huge impact on the lives of those in the workplace. Some examples of such practices of showing care and concern to others include handwritten notes of appreciation, handwritten birthday cards, and shout-outs for marriages, new babies, engagements, and other special events among your team members.

In all of her years as a leader, one thing Barbara always did was write handwritten notes to the team members. She began this practice decades ago. If she saw a job well done or someone had a great day, or even a hard day, she would take a few moments and write a little note of gratitude, sympathy, appreciation, or inspiration. She would mail the card or note to an employee's home address whenever possible. Oftentimes she even put small notes and a treat, like a candy bar, magnet, or other goodie, on each team member's desk after they all went home from work.

Team members were excited about these small acts of kindness. The vibe and the energy were always uplifted when they walked into their offices the next day to a small surprise. Team members love such notes of appreciation. In today's world of high technology, filled with emails or text messages, it is even nicer than ever to get a handwritten card the good old-fashioned way, in the mailbox.

Barbara always received comments of appreciation. These small acts of kindness made her staff happy, just to know someone cared for them. In fact, Barbara walked into one of her remote team member's office one afternoon and her bulletin board was full of all the cards. The board had cards from the previous five years. Barbara laughed and said, "You keep those?" The employee replied that they were her daily inspiration and that she loved them. Further, this employee went on to lead a team and has replicated this best practice.

During the research, Barbara was interviewing university presidents and was shocked to find out that one of the university presidents mailed about 1,500 cards per year to her entire team, most often birthday cards, but also notes of appreciation for a job well done. Sending a few dozen cards a year is great, but to hear hundreds per year! Wow!

That does not even come close to what we found in our research. Douglas Conant, the past CEO of Campbell's Soup, wrote 3,000 cards per year! That's about a dozen cards each work day. Yes, you read that right. Over his ten years as CEO, he is known to have written 30,000 cards to employees. And the best part is that Mr. Conant talks about how these cards also brought him great satisfaction and happiness. Caring for others is very rewarding and brings a piece of comfort to the giver as well as the receiver.

Have you ever received a card from your CEO or president? If you are the president or CEO, have you ever written a card or note, signed by *you*, not your secretary, not a stamp, not a preprinted signature, to each and every employee? Ask yourself, *When was the last time I acknowledged a special event or activity through a handwritten note to each one of my employees?* I challenge CEOs and other top executives to dig deep into this small act of kindness and see how it transforms the culture of the organization.

Another recent example of care and concern comes from an experience of a friend. This woman purchased medical supplies, food, and so on from the company called Chewy.com. After her dog passed away, she called to say she no longer needed the dog's regular shipment. To her surprise, she received a sympathy card in the mail on the loss of her dog.

She was so impressed that she posted the card on social media and provided free advertising in a positive fashion for Chewy.com. This definitely supports a meaning-centered approach to an organization. Chewy.com, a large organization, showed extra care to a customer, and the social media support that followed is sure to have created future profitability for the organization.

In researching if this is a common practice for Chewy.com, endless similar stories were found. Not only do some of the stories mention the cards and flowers being sent, but there were also numerous mentions of how the call center employees provided care and concern by listening deeply to the stories of the grieving pet owners. These small acts of kindness from this large organization are simply heartwarming. Certainly, true customer satisfaction will lead to loyal customers and continued sales for this company. This goes to show that it does not matter how small or large your organization is; care and concern matters to its employees and its customers.

Authentic Connections—MBWA

Another simple, and very practical, way to show care and concern is through authentic connections. Numerous authors have called this Management by Walking Around (MBWA). In fact, Tom Peters, referenced earlier, found MBWA to be one of the greatest success tools of the exemplary organizations back in the 1980s. Again, simple but not put into practice often enough by the leaders in most organizations.

Some may consider this small talk but is actually very big and very important. This small talk shows someone that you care. It involves asking about their home life—*How are the kids? How are your mom and dad? Has your puppy stopped chewing up your shoes yet?* All of these small conversations are meaningful in such an important way. They say to others, "That person really cares about me."

Numerous exemplary leaders interviewed in our studies mentioned how they acknowledge employees with personal small talk briefly before getting to the heart of a conversation. These simple acts of kindness can improve engagement and productivity in your organization. A few probing questions can increase meaning exponentially, and it can take just a couple of brief minutes. It does not have to be a long, drawn-out conversation. Just show you care. But you must be authentic and actively listen if you want this to work.

For a quick pulse-check, ask yourself a few questions about your team members. Do you know how many kids they have? Do you know if they are married, divorced, widowed, single? Do you know their favorite kind of music or ice cream? Is everyone in their family healthy? Do they have pets? Are they taking care of elderly parents or grandparents? Questions like these are all simple, but to how many of these questions can you say yes? Knowing the life stories on a personal level will enable leaders to better understand the person as a whole.

What is even more important is to know what you do not know! One follower in our research defined how important collaboration and wisdom come into play for the day-to-day activities learned through MBWA. She expressed that there is nothing more frustrating than when leadership feels they are sharing wisdom when they have no real experience or personal insight into what is happening on the front line. The people on the front line know what is happening and it cannot be faked by the leader. A leader cannot act omnipotent without demonstrating their level of true knowledge of what is happening at all levels. MBWA allows a leader to live out that knowledge and gain insight into each person's position. These examples can be learned by walking around, observing, and listening with intention.

Our research found that followers described an environment of trust as an environment where everyone is focused on a common purpose and led by someone who shows that they care about them. Trusting and caring behavior is not only valued by followers but essential to uniting followers around a common purpose. We will talk more about uniting followers around a common purpose in Part II, but it is essential to see the interplay between engagement and empowerment. In fact, even our third E, expertise, had interplay with caring. How you express your expertise is clearly linked to caring behavior. Of the respondents in our research, 77.5 percent claimed that a leader's ability to show concern for others was very important or critically important to how they expressed their wisdom. Similarly, those followers also ranked leaders' behaviors that show they care above the mean.

We hope by now you see how the interplay of engagement, empowerment, and expertise flow from similar wellsprings. The waters of that spring are your followers yearning for meaning. As a leader, you can begin the journey toward becoming a maker of meaning by starting with building trust and having care and concern for your followers. Trusting relationships, marked by care and concern, are the key to these foundational building blocks of creating meaning for yourself and your followers within your organizations.

We also hope that you will consider taking steps to build care and concern in your organization. First, consider an open-door policy that allows your followers to approach you on an as-needed basis. Just as you approach them when you need to communicate issues important to the organization, employees need the opportunity to approach leadership with issues important to them. Second, take the time for individual conversations that show you care about your people as individuals. If that behavior can impact a Marine Corps. Infantry platoon, it can certainly impact your organization. Third, take the time to send personal notes that celebrate the individual. Finally, develop your relationships by walking around and connecting directly with your team members. Those few moments on the part of the leader build the connective undercurrent needed for meaning to grow.

Reflection Questions for Care and Concern

How I demonstrate my accessibility and open-door policy includes:

Specific ways I connect with others in their workspace include:

Specific ways I demonstrate genuine care include:

I recognize others in the workplace by:

How many notes of appreciation have I sent this week, month, year?

Chapter 6

Open Communication with Active Listening

True listening builds strength in other people.

—Robert K. Greenleaf, *Servant Leadership*

Open communication with active listening is essential to building strong relationships and higher engagement within your organization. Through open communication with active listening, leaders can communicate character and deepen organizational relationships.

Followers rank open communication with active listening as critically important. When responding to questions about how their leader expresses character, over 80 percent of followers in the study rated "actively listens when communicating with others" as very important or critically important. Leaders must not only "hear" what is being said but "actively listen" and engage with employees to create meaningful engagement in the workplace.

The exemplary leaders interviewed in our research did voice similar beliefs about the importance of engagement through communication but, unfortunately, did not rank the need for active listening as highly as did the followers. The disconnect between the leader's perception and the follower's perception of the need to actively listen is evident. Followers are begging their leaders to actively listen more, yet leaders did not respond that it was critical. It is imperative leaders learn this much requested skill as your followers are craving it.

Leaders and followers alike understood the need for strong relationships that optimize opportunities for innovation, change, and growth. One leader added, "Without trusting relationships there is a fear of failure." This leader expressed failure as a necessary precursor to innovation. The leaders further described coaching and ongoing team building as processes necessary to build relationships that help to create a innovative company. Their words expressed the necessity of building and maintaining strong relationships as a necessary and important part of their leadership: "everyone speaks," "relationships lead to engagement," and "we have to engage people to make them feel welcome, like they are part of the family."

The essential need for strong relationships that the exemplary leaders expressed in our research was also found in their discussion of communicating and building character in their companies. All the leaders seemingly acknowledged their role in building character—character building that was made possible by strong relationships and deep follower engagement. This interplay of trusting relationships and character building leading to engagement helps to clarify the complexity of the task. Engagement requires constant attention to the quality of your relationships. They must be built on a strong foundation of trust, if leaders hope to build character and create teams that are willing and able to adapt to change and become innovative. Listening to others builds a trusting foundation for relationships to develop and the leaders' characters to be expressed.

One thing is clear: the leaders in our research do value communication. They clearly connected communication to building relationships and expressing their character. We would stress that leaders need to ensure their definition of communication contains an understanding and ability to focus on the receptive end of communication as well. Without this important skill, leaders may miss an opportunity to communicate important information and build the type of relationships needed for deep engagement.

Across a variety of industries, the exemplary leaders expressed the importance of listening. One exemplary leader described that listening shows that you are available for your followers. That leader added a caveat that listening does not mean that the follower always walks away with a changed outcome, but it is important that they were listened to. Similarly, another exemplary CEO expressed that leaders need to ensure that team members know their voices matter. Perhaps the need to listen is best summed up by the exemplary leaders who expressed the need to hear what others think and ensure they are not doing all the talking.

Creating collaborative practices is one of the ways the exemplary leaders ensured that their organizational teams had an opportunity to listen to each other. These practices not only ensure listening but give teams the time to calibrate actions and move together. One of the exemplary leaders clarified a statement about the team by describing the collective *we*. It is that collaborative collective *we* that leads to engagement, and it is the collective garden where meaning grows best.

Consider the following example from *Built to Last*, by Jim Collins and Jerry Porras. In speaking about Hewlett Packard (HP), they described an environment where open communication was valued:

It was also one of the first American companies to introduce an open-door policy in which employees could bring grievances all the way to the top without retribution. To promote communication and informality and to deemphasize hierarchy, HP created a wide-open floor plan; no manager at any level would be allowed to have a private office with a door—a very unusual practice in the 1950s.[1]

Collins and Porras set out to identify what makes high-performing companies different from other companies. In the case of HP, it seems establishing opportunities for open communication was part of the fiber of the company. HP did more than just create transparency; they created an environment that allowed engagement to be fostered through open communication. The need to be listened to and be in relationships with others at work is vital to creating meaning.

Relationships can be both an antecedent and a path toward engagement and meaning-making. Author Scott Mautz substantiated via research the role that relationships play in helping others create meaning. He cited research that concluded, "relationships are not just vehicles to help further career goals, but rather are rich sources of meaning in and of themselves."[2]

Active listening does much more than just build an environment conducive to positive workplace relationships; it provides opportunities to have crucial conversations that can be pivotal to your leadership success. Kegan and Lahey, authors of *How the Way We Talk Can Change the Way We Work*, described active listening as one of the most important conversational skills a person can develop. They suggested that active listening is about taking up temporary residence in the other's meaning. They clarified, "Actually, active listening is not about supporting the other's position. It is about supporting the language space, so a deconstructive conversation can ensue."[3]

The idea is not to silence all conflict through harmonious active listening sessions. It is to build an environment of trust where conversations, even those that may present conflict, can take place. In this dynamic tension, conflict can be deconstructed to lead to enhanced outcomes and the promotion of workplace meaning.

Similarly, McMillan and Switzler, the authors of *Crucial Conversations: Tools for Talking When Stakes Are High*, suggested that when nobody is listening, everyone is committed to silence or violence, leaving the pool of shared meaning tainted and parched. They illustrated skills for listening called "power listening tools," using the acronym AMPP: Ask, Mirror, Paraphrase, and Prime. They described these tools as useful for either violence or silence. According to the authors, the easiest path to action is simply inviting others to express themselves. They offered:

In order for people to move from acting on their feelings to talking about their conclusions and observations, we must listen in a way that makes it safe for others to share their intimate thoughts. They must believe that when they share their thoughts, they won't offend others or be punished for speaking frankly.[4]

One clear corporate example was from a sales team that went completely silent after numerous reorganizations. At first, the sales team was excited about the new opportunity for change. Incentives were promised, new materials were slated to be ordered, territories were rearranged, accounts were designated, and leadership shifted.

The sales team embraced the changes at first, and they looked forward to what was to come, but then the changes continued. The incentive program never got off the ground, the territories continued to change, the team leads changed numerous times, job descriptions and roles changed, positions were not posted, people were promoted without the opportunities for others to apply, and ultimately chaos ensued.

As the sales team pushed back, the leadership team pushed back even harder. Employees started to complain, the number of resignations increased, employees were going out on medical stress leave, and the communication declined significantly. In fact, as one individual asked a question, the team member was completely berated in front of the entire team, which made the other team members recoil and become even more silent. Eventually, everyone succumbed to just keeping their heads down. As one long time employee said, *I'm keeping my head down so it doesn't get chopped off!*

Meaning and purpose were completely destroyed. Trust had been broken. Hope was diminished and the team struggled to recover. Leadership team members were not listening; more specifically, leadership was not hearing or processing the concerns of the team members. The team was crumbling due to a lack of open and honest communication with active listening. Open communication dwindled due to the erosion of trust. Recovery in this situation could take years to accomplish.

Active listening not only allows for crucial conversations to take place, it also allows the building of trusting relationships and enables a leader to express care and concern. Perhaps more importantly, it creates an opportunity for leaders to teach followers. As mentioned at the outset of this chapter, when people are focused on accomplishing a complex task, they find meaning. This deeper level of speaking and listening is necessary for a leader to engage followers in the learning required when working on complex tasks.

Ulrich and Ulrich, authors of *The Why of Work*, described this as the synergy that happens when human relationships are at their best. Meaningful relationships enhance a feeling of abundance and allow leaders to build cohesive and high-performing teams. Furthermore, Kouzes and Posner offered that these teaching opportunities between leader and follower allow for relationships to rise to a level of profound interactions.

The essential need for strong relationships that the exemplary leaders expressed in our research was also found in their discussion of communicating and building character in their companies. All the leaders acknowledged their role in building character. Character building was made possible by strong relationships and deep follower engagement.

This interplay of trusting relationships and character building, which leads to engagement, helps to clarify the complexity of the task. Engagement requires constant attention to the quality of your relationships, which must be built on a strong foundation of trust and constant communication if leaders hope to build character and create teams that are willing and able to adapt to change and become innovative.

> Trust is the social glue that binds human relationships.
>
> —James Kouzes and Barry
> Posner, *A Leader's Legacy*

In their book *A Leader's Legacy*, James Kouzes and Barry Posner stated: "Our leaders, then, are most likely to be people we're closest to and know more intimately. We're just more likely to trust people we know, to work harder for people we know, to do our best for people we know, to commit to people we know, and to follow people we know."[5] They go on to state that leaders who treat their followers with dignity and respect see significantly higher performance. With that in mind, consider their claim, "Leadership is a relationship." The vast majority of us do not choose relationships with people who do not validate us and make us feel significant. The same is true of your leadership relationships.

The fastest way to destroy trust and alienate your followers is to communicate in ways that do not allow for a reciprocal relationship to take place. It is even worse is to communicate in ways that are incongruent with actions. To build that closeness all communication must be two-way and allow for active listening.

Consider the description Kouzes and Posner state when they say the leader-constituent relationship is one which requires a resounding connection with followers, including matters that relate to the heart. In the same chapter they explain, "The requirement is to assemble a team of individuals who can vigorously express their differences while also energetically moving in unison toward an ennobling future."[6] When you think of the dynamics of the modern-day workplace, with diverse teams and individuals with strong opinions, this leadership challenge can seem daunting. Establishing a caring environment marked by open communication with active listening is a way to ensure your teams can express their opinions while focusing on the larger goals of your organization.

STRATEGIES FOR SUCCESS

Clearly, the importance of communication with true active listening is vital to creating a meaning-centered workplace. Like care and concern, active listening and engaging in open and honest communication are soft skills that are often overlooked. An honest self-assessment of your true listening skills is vital to your success. Below are some simple strategies for success to build your communication and listening skills, including practicing transparency, developing collaboration, and a tip called "ARE you listening?," which will help you hone in on your listening skills.

Practice Transparency

Critical information should be shared throughout the organization. The open-door policy established in chapter 5 is a good first step, but outgoing information must also be shared regularly. Any information that will be shared with the public must be shared with employees, directly from organizational leaders, prior to release to the general public.

Furthermore, identify the ways your employees communicate and include a variety of communication methods. The communication plan can be aided by a communication audit. Consider an established format as your organization's electronic bulletin board. Whether you provide a monthly missive or a weekly update, these messages need to be readily available to all employees, likely through a repository on the company's intranet.

Create a mechanism for sharing important information in a timely manner. If you find yourself asking others, "Did you read your email?" you probably need to reconsider how you share important information. The avenues for sharing information today are endless and must be appropriate for all generations working in the workforce. A leader's attempt at open communication will likely fall short if they are not cognizant of the communication needs of their multigenerational workforces. Communication can be conveyed through email, social media, group messages, intranet, or any other common mode of communication within your organization.

To be transparent, a leader must know the communication needs of their employees. Simply using a text message group chat or a message-sharing app like WhatsApp can provide you the opportunity to get information out. Social media provides another opportunity to share information through closed groups. Today's employees are used to accessing social media for this purpose, so it makes sense that your social media channels provide information that is relevant for their development and understanding of organizational actions.

360° Assessments and Communication Audits

Leaders should seriously consider conducting a variety of 360° Assessments and communication audits, at a minimum annually, to honestly assess the perceptions of your followers as it relates to your listening skills. As found in our research, it is often common for there to be inconsistencies in the scores of how you believe you are listening as opposed to the perception your followers have on your listening skills. Uncovering these truths is very important in knowing how you can grow and improve your listening skills.

Furthermore, 360° Assessments should be performed with each key leader within his or her own functional department annually. Team members must be able to evaluate each individual leader separately and anonymously. By allowing confidential input on a leader's skills and abilities on a regular basis, team members will feel the environment is safe for truthful comments. Upon reviewing the results, coaching plans can be put into place for areas that need coaching, and celebrations can take place for areas in which a leader excels. Senior management can also capitalize on the strengths of exemplary leaders by having them coach others on strong traits and characteristics. Coaching and mentoring can be an ongoing process if open and honest feedback is allowed to be shared on a regular basis.

Develop Collaborative Practices

Relationships between departments and teams need to be encouraged by formal and informal collaborative practices. Creating time and the expectation that teams share vital workflow information is essential. Consider the communication methods that teams use to share information. Try bringing teams or team leaders together for sharing information. This helps to build a culture of open communication.

The trust-building activities we shared in chapter 4 will help create teams that will openly share information. To have true transparency and open communication, all members of the organization need to be willing and able to share pertinent information. A leader sets that habit in place by practicing open communication and creating opportunities for collaboration. By building team connections and trust, a leader can establish a culture that encourages informal collaboration to take place on an ongoing basis; however, formal collaboration should also be considered as a way to ensure open communication throughout the organization.

ARE You Listening?

We offer a simple model to ensure you are actively listening to your employees: ARE you listening:

Attention
Reflection
Elaboration

By simply asking yourself, ARE you listening, you can remember to follow three basics of active communication. Start by paying 100 percent attention to the speaker. That means physically and mentally. You need to eliminate other distractions and face the speaker. If you are engaged in other tasks, put them on hold. That signifies to the listener that you are fully ready, willing, and able to listen to them. Use body language that communicates you are 100 percent present: lean in, maintain eye contact, and nod your head to show you are listening.

Reflect what you are hearing. The simple act of restating what others say to you shows you are listening, and it lessens the possibility for miscommunication. Validate others' statements. Try using statements that reiterate what was said to show you understand the feeling behind their words; a simple "Okay, I see" goes a long way in building validation with others.

Elaborate on what you are hearing. Ask probing questions to take the conversation to a deeper level. You may be able to uncover the needed information. Consider the scenario where an employee wants to vent about another employee's performance. It would build distrust and be inappropriate to show validation of this type of behind-the-back discussion. However, if you do not respond, this situation will likely fester. By elaborating, you can gain useful information to help you better understand the issue.

A case in point: Ed recently had a female employee approach him about a male employee on a performance/behavioral issue. His initial thought was, "We are all adults here; why don't you speak with that person yourself?" As he listened and asked for that person to elaborate, he learned they had a history. Additional conversations proved this was not an isolated experience. With that information, he was able to have a deeper conversation that not only resolved the issue but also helped the male employee correct his behavior. Both conversations were crucial for the culture of the organization. One supported an employee and the other helped an employee reflect on their behavior and grow.

The point is, by not taking time to listen carefully, you may miss opportunities to address issues that will then be left to fester. In the situation described, only rancor and discord would have followed. Instead, there is now a clear understanding of what is expected in terms of interpersonal communication that is respectful. Both employees benefited, and so did the organizational culture.

It is not enough that you possess the skills required for actively communicating. You must also ensure your teams can communicate effectively. In the scenario previously mentioned, a potential rift between coworkers was prevented, but the real lesson learned was that a leader must work every day to ensure all team members can communicate effectively with each other. The exemplary leaders in our studies described the need to actively coach their employees to communicate effectively.

Open-Ended Questions

An excellent activity to teach others about effective communication is to practice role-playing based on open-ended questioning. This type of questioning can feel very uncomfortable at first, but through practice and repetition, the exercise becomes easier, and one will find that the conversations in which they engage will become more meaningful.

For this activity, teams will break into groups of two. Each member of the group writes the name of a famous person on a card. In round one, the two members take turns asking closed-ended questions: yes or no. One person can keep asking probing questions for as long as the answer remains yes. When the answer is no, the other person takes over, asking questions. For example, you may ask, *Am I alive? Am I male? Do I play sports? Do I sing?* After ten to fifteen minutes, stop the activity. By this time, some of the people will have guessed their partner's famous person, while others may not have been able to come up with the answer, and that's okay.

In round two, the partners will think of two more famous people, write them on their cards, and not reveal them to their partners. This time the team members may only ask open-ended questions, meaning the questions must describe or explain more about the individual. These types of questions include examples like *Explain what you do for a living, Describe your looks,* and *Tell me about your favorite activities.* If someone asked a closed-ended yes-or-no question, they must forfeit their turn. Continued probing questions help the interviewee to keep talking. The conversation goes deep and meaning is established. This forces the conversation to continue, a true conversation to ensue, and a relationship to be built.

This activity shows that more information is gleaned about a person if open-ended questions are asked. Oftentimes people find it much easier to ask closed-ended questions, but more information is gathered and synthesized, providing you the ability to go deeper, through open-ended questioning. Again, this is not an easy task, so it is important to practice and role play with a coach or a colleague to get skilled at open-ended questioning. Try this in your regular day-to-day conversations. Ask probing, open-ended questions to go deeper into your relationships. It is not easy at first, but keep practicing and it will become more comfortable over time.

Can You Hear Me?

It is not enough to just listen. An exemplary leader will also understand and *hear* what is being messaged through words, actions, body language, and subliminal messages. *"ARE you listening?"* is a great technique to ensure that you are listening deeply—paying attention, reflecting, and elaborating in the conversation, but it is also critical to let team members know you truly "hear" what is being said. Hearing is the deeper part of listening and allows one to process exactly what is being stated with a clear direction of the next steps. Process, understand, validate, and support team members by truly hearing them.

There is a saying attributed to author Robert McCloskey that reads, *"I know that you believe you understand what you think I said, but I'm not sure you realize that what you heard is not what I meant."* This is a perfect summation of "hearing" versus "listening." The keywords are "what you heard is not what I meant." A very serious and relevant strategy for success in communication and active listening is memorizing and implementing this saying. Find out what they meant! Ensure that your message is not only heard but validate that the recipient understands the message and that its meaning is accurate.

By hearing, team members are ensured that what was communicated is actually understood by the recipient. This is an ongoing process within the communication cycle. Validation and clarification of all steps of a conversation are critical. This takes elaboration to a level of implementation. While practicing hearing, elaborate on the conversation deeply. An example may look like this:

> What I am hearing you say is you like the direction we are taking, but you would like to see XYZ. X is this. Y is that. Is there any more information you can give me to describe X, Y and Z? How can we help implement these strategies? What does that look like?

Conversations like this should be ongoing. Again, use open-ended questioning to ensure accuracy of the communication. Any type of validation opportunity is good when conversing with others as everyone is coming to a conversation from a different space. It is important that the conversation be understood by all in the room and that patience is part of the conversation to ensure everyone is on the same page. Further, exemplary leaders are skilled at reading body language and facial expressions, so be sure to both listen and hear what is being said by paying attention to the full person.

Establishing open communication with active listening as an essential interpersonal communication protocol is necessary for it to be practiced organization wide. It would be greatly distracting as a leader if you spent all your time solving interpersonal communication issues; however, by modeling positive interpersonal dialogue that uses the "ARE you listening?" and "I hear you" techniques, you can begin to model expectations through your own actions. As a result, similar behaviors from other team members will follow and continue to spread throughout the organization.

Reflection Questions for Communication and Active Listening

My primary communication methods for sharing vital information are:

How do I ensure I actively listen and use the ARE approach?

Specific ways the office space is conducive to collaboration and creative
   communication:

The ways I can improve upon my open communication within the organization are:

SUMMARY OF ENGAGEMENT

Part I offered a framework for understanding the importance of establishing trust, care, and concern as foundational requirements for building the resonant relationships leaders need with followers. We have also shown that communication is enhanced when it is transparent and two-way. Your leadership communication is incomplete unless it includes actively listening to your followers. The foundational elements of engagement are trust, care and concern, and open communication with active listening.

Engagement can strengthen your leadership and provide opportunities for meaning to be created. Engaged teams can accomplish any mission. Your greatest organizational and personal missions can be accomplished if you lead highly engaged teams. We will return to engagement as we discuss ways to measure and reflect on the deep engagement with your followers. You will also see the necessity for deeply engaged teams as we discuss empowerment and expertise as all the elements of the 3Es work together to create a meaning-centered culture.

In Part II we will look at the way leaders empower their followers to create a collaborative vision and an inspired workforce. It starts with the deep engagement, created by building trusting relationships achieved through open communication with active listening, and is supported by the elements of empowerment, including leading with collaborative visioning, recognition, and enthusiasm.

Part II

EMPOWERMENT

My job as a leader is to make sure that everybody in the company has great opportunities and they feel they are having meaningful impact to the good of society.

—Larry Page, Google

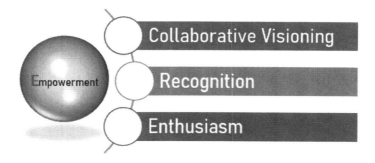

Elements of Empowerment.

The greatest gift you can give to your followers is empowerment – empowering them to work on a goal that is challenging and complex. Meaning is made in this fertile ground where seeds of trust via empowerment are planted. By creating an inspirational vision of a future worth striving for, leaders can begin to create a bridge from the present to the future. This bridge of empowerment must be built through collaborative visioning, enthusiasm, and recognition. Nothing is stronger than an empowered team working enthusiastically toward a common vision of an inspiring future.

In Part I we outlined steps for engaging followers. In Part II we look at the deeper engagement and commitment found in empowerment. The trusting relationships and open communication you establish will allow you to have a deep understanding of your followers' strengths, skills, and opinions.

Before reading the chapters on empowerment, consider how you currently empower your employees. Jot down your empowerment practices. Consider the behaviors and strategies you use to empower your team members. Be as honest as you can on these reflective questions so that your self-assessment is meaningful to your personal development. You can even have discussions with a confidant or friend about their perception of your empowerment capabilities.

Reflection Questions for Empowerment

The current ways I empower my colleagues include:

Specific ways the organization creates opportunities for recognition include:

Ways that I excite and empower team members include:

Recognizing success is spontaneous and can be seen when:

Ways that I can display enthusiasm include:

According to Gallup, when measuring employee engagement, workplace elements are assessed with clear links to performance outcomes: opportunities for workers to do what they do best, to develop their job skills, and to have their opinions count. In a 2018 Gallup Poll report, worker engagement was recorded at an eighteen-year high, yet they still cited employee engagement at dismal levels of 53 percent of workers being in the not engaged category and 17 percent being in the actively disengaged category. More importantly, Gallup research has found that nearly 70 percent of the variance in team engagement is explained by the quality of the manager or team leader. By creating a collaborative vision, using recognition and personal enthusiasm, leaders can empower their followers and deepen the engagement and commitment of their teams.

Chapter 7

Collaborative Visioning

Taking the time to think through and articulate common purpose brings clarity in place of confusion, wholeness in place of unrelated fragment.

—John Varney, Chief Executive,
Center for Management Creativity

A vision creates the bridge from the present state of an organization to a future state of the organization. To ensure buy-in from all stakeholders, the vision must be developed as a team. Building the vision collaboratively allows the team to sustain higher levels of motivation in maintaining the vision. Through collaborative visioning, the team will also be assured of withstanding organizational challenges as they arise. Collaborative visioning will allow the team to create higher meaning and purpose in all that they do by setting their sights and goals on the overall vision and mission of the organization. It is imperative a leader provide a bullseye at which the team can aim.

Prior to developing the vision, the leader and the team must review the current state of the organization: Is the organization prepared to develop a new or revised vision for the future? Will stakeholders be collaborative, cooperative, and supportive of a new vision? Is the employee engagement high or low? Are employee relationships strong enough for open and honest dialogue about the vision to take place?

Positive relationships among employees will ensure success and sustainability of the vision. Employees and other stakeholders must be in an environment of safety and authenticity to be assured that all ideas while developing the collaborative vision will be considered and respected. It is through these relationships that open dialogue can take place when building, and later supporting, the vision. A strong leader will ensure everyone's concentration remains focused on this overall vision.

The vision must be well-defined, with objectives and steps to ensure understanding from team members. It is not enough, though, to just create a vision; the vision must be a constant lived experience. Even a great leader cannot support the vision alone. It must be supported by all team members and must be woven throughout the organization, from the entry-level positions to top leadership. This collaborative visioning will lead to creating meaning among team members throughout the organization.

In the *Change Leader's Roadmap*, Ackerman-Anderson and Anderson suggested that "there is no greater accelerator of change than people who have a shared vision they are collectively committed to creating."[1] The exemplary leaders interviewed in our research indicated that while they took responsibility for their company vision, they all included their teams in co-creating and maintaining that vision. They suggested that their ability to innovate and change depended on a fully shared vision. Again, back to listening and hearing, it is critical that leaders and team members communicate openly. It is important to validate the perceptions of the shared vision and the plans for follow-through. The worst situation is to have a leader say, "This is what you asked for, wouldn't you agree?" and for the team members to resoundingly disagree but be too afraid to speak up.

An effective vision must excite and empower others and, to do so, all stakeholders must be included in the visioning process. All stakeholders succeed when effectively using the vision to communicate the goals and the road map to success. An operative vision presents a compelling view of the future: a view that clarifies the direction forward. For a vision to be effective, it must have the characteristics that serve to bring a team together around a new future that both excites and empowers them in a meaningful way. Furthermore, as stated by Kouzes and Posner, "Leaders have to enlist others in a common vision . . . . Leaders breathe life into the hopes and dreams of others and enable them to see the exciting possibilities that the future holds"[2] A leader develops a sense of overall purpose within the organization.

Author Peter Senge theorized as early as 2004 that future leadership would be driven by teams of collective leadership. Similarly, Ackerman-Anderson and Anderson agreed thus when they invoked this collective-leadership idea in 2001: "Our recommendation is that stakeholders be involved in building the vision of their future, along with executive guidance."[3] They explained that leaders who create a vision in isolation slow down the development of collective ownership of new ideas. This collaborative visioning process is ongoing. It is important to connect tangible actions of daily tasks on all levels and emphasize how they build toward the vision of the organization. Today, more than ever, employees are seeking to find their connection and purpose in the work they do daily. When employees understand the connection of their daily actions to the overall purpose of their position, engagement and empowerment are increased.

The need to have a clear and compelling vision is irrefutable. In fact, as stated in Proverbs 29:18, "Where there is no vision, the people perish." By developing a vision with followers, you create a collaborative mindset. That mindset is needed for teams to work in collaboration, where innovation can flourish and meaning can be constructed. Leaders are challenged to help their followers find a higher purpose to their work, to help them find meaning.

That deep organizational clarity can be found in a collaborative vision that members feel a part of creating and sustaining. And it is important to recognize that everyone in every position has a connection to, and responsibility for, relating their daily activities to the overall vision—from the administrative assistant's role in keeping leaders on task to the call center personnel who are at the frontlines of customer satisfaction. It is important to build this role clarity and to help others recognize that everyone's role and purpose varies, and that without them, like the bearings on a wheel, the whole cannot function without all parts working together.

The key to driving innovation, growth, and commitment is tied to a leader's ability to create a collaborative vision with the team members and continue to drive team members toward the common vision in all that they do. The exemplary technology leaders interviewed during our research indicated that vision was one of the most important elements of their leadership. One leader stated plainly, "If you can't explain your vision, you are dead in the water." This leader later elaborated that the CEO's job was to create the feeling of a team that sees the vision all the time, and that weekly meetings were essentially vision sessions. Another exemplary leader stated, "If you don't give people a vision of where you're going, you wind up with resistance to change." "Vision creates direction for everyone," stated a third leader.

As one of the exemplary leaders in our research explained, vision is an ongoing and collaborative feature of their weekly meetings. When a leader takes time to develop a vision that maximizes buy-in and connects tangible actions to meet that goal, they increase their meaning-making ability. This was supported by what Peter Senge shared in 2006 when he discussed how loyalty comes from a shared vision and is inspired not by an idea but by a true force in people's hearts.

The multifaceted leaders represented in the meaning research all expressed how fundamentally necessary vision is to their work. They described the need for the vision to be shared for several important reasons. One exemplary leader expressed that the vision contains the everyday values of the organization. Another leader described that when the vision is a shared vision, engagement is easier to achieve. An exemplary CEO described codeveloping the vision to create excitement for the future while developing passion and inspiration among their followers.

The exemplary leaders also expressed an understanding that market influences constantly create the need for the vision to change. One CEO described vision as an ever-changing journey. This statement ties into the imperative that several of the exemplary leaders mentioned—the need to never be content with where you are and to constantly be looking forward. In this sense, the exemplary leaders suggest that the vision simultaneously must meet the needs of the present, while being able to pivot as market forces demand.

The lack of having a collaborative vision comes with a "fire, aim, ready" approach, instead of a "ready, aim, fire" approach. Without a collaborative vision, leaders often spend more time putting out fires than preparing appropriately to avoid fires. This undue stress has team members scrambling to make each of these fires a priority, and everything becomes urgent and rushed, causing undue stress and frustrations. Without active listening, the leader does not hear the warnings from the team members who are at the forefront of the market. Instead, in one case the follower said that warnings were provided, but the leader was dismissive and not hearing what was shared. By developing the vision collaboratively, a solid plan and preparations could be made to meet the needs of what the team members are experiencing in the field.

Developing a vision and connecting it to tangible actions is only part of the leadership task in creating a collaborative vision. The vision also needs to be communicated in an inspirational fashion. An exemplary leader in our research explained that he told "stories from the field." Bringing back stories of customer satisfaction to teams working on product development was his way of providing inspirational stories so teams could see the impact of their efforts. One leader shared the story of the company founding and growth to build background and help new employees see the trajectory of the company. Building this collective understanding of the company vision via storytelling is an effective practice. Through storytelling, leaders are able to develop transparency and allow the vision to help followers develop meaning. That sense of meaning is found in the hope of a brighter future and is a task worth pursuing.

Perhaps no one is better at creating a shared vision than Elon Musk. In his announcement of the Model Y, he reviewed the story of the company. He pointed out their successes in rocketry and solar power development to support the launch of a new vehicle. The story led to the bigger idea of creating a sustainable future—a future so limitless that colonizing Mars is a plausible goal. For everyone in the Tesla family, the message was loud and clear: your work is important! The engineers, rocket scientists, assemblers, and programmers working for Musk understand that compelling vision. They have become part of the collaborative team delivering the future.

Similar to Elon Musk and the sharing of the vision and goals of the organization, storytelling is a visionary's way of explaining the vision for the future. In *the Leader's Guide to Storytelling*, Stephen Denning explains the way in which leadership storytelling is a naturally collaborative process and can inspire the team to the shared vision. He suggests that when a leader operates from an interactive mode, there is no reason to be submissive or rebellious. He states that it is not important for a listener to accept or reject the story, but it is a way to bring the audience and goal together. It is a mutually shared experience.

Denning goes on to describe the need for interactive leaders to listen and interact with their followers. He describes the interactive leadership model, accompanied by narrative tools, as one that fits a modern need. It is through conversation and collaboration that team members feel validated and recognized for their work in supporting the vision. When leaders interact with followers and listen to stories about lived experiences of the vision, follower empowerment increases. The narrative or storytelling ability of leadership can be a very powerful leadership tool to express a compelling vision.

Vision is often described as a tool that leaders use to show the way forward to a compelling future. Product innovation and team commitment are greatly influenced by the leaders' ability to use vision as an antecedent for action. When your goals are clearly articulated in an inspirational vision that others feel a part of, then the future state can be created. Consider again the work of Collins and Porras. They described creating a Big Hairy Audacious Goal (BHAG) in order to create bold goals with clarity. Now consider the goal of creating a sustainable future and colonizing Mars. The goals that Elon Musk has set for his organization are indeed BHAGs.

One of the most compelling national BHAGs was put in motion in 1961. On May 25, 1961, President John F. Kennedy delivered a speech to a joint session of congress. That speech declared a BHAG for America's space exploration program, a declaration of intention to put a man on the moon. On July 20, 1969, that dream was realized when Neil Armstrong stepped onto the surface of the moon.

President Kennedy's speech in 1961 made it clear that the battle against tyranny was inextricably linked to our space program. He stated the importance clearly, "Now it is time to take longer strides—time for a great new American enterprise—time for this nation to take a clearly leading role in space achievement, which in many ways may hold the key to our future on earth."

President Kennedy not only tied this BHAG to our very survival; he described what was needed: "every scientist, every engineer, every serviceman, every technician, contractor, and civil servant gives his personal pledge that this nation will move forward, with the full speed of freedom, in the exciting adventure of space." And he stated optimistically he believed it could be done: "I believe we possess all the resources and talents necessary." Kennedy's BHAG inspired a nation to believe that every American was important to impact the vision.

A BHAG serves as a mechanism to spur change, innovation, and progress. Beyond altering an organization's course, BHAGs create a focus that helps others find meaning. Even if you do not possess the oratory skills of President Kennedy, you can create your own organizational BHAG by following the steps President Kennedy used in his address to congress.

- Declare the needed change.
- State what each individual must do.
- Affirm the outcome.

Striving for a challenging future state is what one needs to find meaning in one's life and in one's work. Even if your organizational change is smaller in scope than building rockets, you can follow the steps listed above to help your organization make change and find meaning.

Collaborative visioning can also be used for making incremental change within an organization. Incremental changes to a vision are always needed to adjust to market forces, technological changes, vision expansion, and other factors. This type of change can follow steps similar to those listed above; however, we outline several steps to create a collaborative mindset among your followers.

Once an area of change is identified, engage others in possibility thinking. By challenging your followers to imagine the possibility of a new future brought about by change, you begin to future-cast the organization as if the change has occurred. You will also create an opportunity for dialogue around key features of the change that will likely impact others. This important step allows you to provide information that develops organizational understanding of why the change is needed and how others will benefit.

The buy-in of key team members prior to declaring the needed change will dramatically impact the effectiveness of your vision for organizational change. In order for a declaration of change to move the organization forward, you must have buy-in. President Kennedy consulted with his vice president, lead NASA administrators, and other key officials prior to his declaration before congress. Ensuring buy-in is essential to carrying out a change that you are asking others to implement.

In a recent leadership consultation, a leader stated, "I am beginning to question my leadership." That leader was getting resistance from key leadership team members during the initial implementation phase of a process change. By declaring the change without considering the impact on the people closest to carrying out the nuts and bolts of managing the change, the leader faced the difficult task of managing change without the support of all members of the leadership team. It is imperative to make change transparent and collaborative.

Consider a scenario of an organization that does not have buy-in from important stakeholders. This is a common theme, especially among sales and marketing teams. Marketing departments oftentimes pivot in direction without consulting feedback of the team on the frontline. Sales teams feel their changes would be for different reasons than marketing. Sales blames marketing, marketing blames sales. Instead of hearing conversations about market shifts, one makes changes without buy-in, support, and feedback from the other. Once the teams are in conflict, support for the vision declines.

After engaging your team in possibility thinking, it is time to begin mapping the change to identify the second step. Identifying and stating what each individual must do should take place as a collaborative conversation. Envisioning change without considering what changes each individual must make will create the potential for derailment. If you are working with a leadership team that must manage the change, they need the opportunity to understand their role in supervising all tasks that support that change. Once you have identified the details of what each individual must do, you are ready for the final step.

Affirming the outcome of the vision is a leader's constant demand. Whether it is the overall vision or a course correction, leaders must affirm the outcome while addressing concerns. If your people have the tools they need and a vision that constantly pulls them forward through affirming the outcome, they will deliver. Think of the obstacles that faced the first NASA team. They managed to deliver on President Kennedy's original BHAG that affirmed all the talents and resources were in place.

Even if your goal is not as big as landing on the moon, focusing on the key elements of the vision and inviting others to collaborate in its development and implementation is essential. Start with possibility thinking: clearly identify what each individual must do. Continue to modify, adjust, and refine along the way. Affirm the outcome. These steps are sure to help the team bring the vision to life, but remember, the vision must always be addressed. Even in a mature organization with a long-standing vision, it is important that the organization continue to define the vision loud and clear.

The bedrock for the foundation of any company is only as strong as its vision. Once the envisioned future and the company values are illuminated, the heavy lifting of ensuring organizational commitment to that vision is essential. The leader must succinctly and passionately communicate the organization's vision, moving everyone forward toward a common, compelling, and tangible future. A collaborative vision should continually inspire and solidify everyone's organizational commitment and identity. The vision must never die, or so too will the organization. This inspiring and ongoing organizational commitment to the vision will allow a sense of meaning to be generated from the day-to-day work.

STRATEGIES FOR SUCCESS

Below you will find tried-and-true strategies to support the implementation and sustainment of a collaborative vision. Remember, it is vital the leadership team communicate clearly to stakeholders about why an organization does what it does. The building of a collaborative vision ensures buy-in from all team members. A vision is sustainable when it is co-created with team members and when all team members consistently remind each other of the vision. Furthermore, before others can follow, leaders need to show themselves living out the vision. Leaders must embrace the vision and help employees to embrace the vision, making it more viable and sustainable.

Free Flow of Communication

It is imperative that the vision is communicated often, in an honest and authentic manner. From training and development to coaching and collaboration, there are ways to support the vision to allow for ease of communication between employees. This includes creating environments for casual conversations. Most have likely heard of the term "water cooler conversations." It is here where authentic and creative conversations take place. When an organization has break rooms and common areas for team members to relax and converse, authenticity prevails. By setting up these common areas, and allowing team members to go into the common areas at any time during the day, true conversations can develop. The free flow of these conversations encourages and inspires team members toward a common goal of developing the vision.

Share the Vision

The next important strategy for success is sharing the vision. It is a best practice among exemplary leaders to state the vision statement on websites, in marketing materials, through internal memos, and perhaps even through a reward program whereby people are recognized specifically for tasks relating to sharing the corporate vision.

Some organizations in the research even had the vision posted on or near the main office. Others had bulletin boards with the headline of the shared vision and then success stories that aligned with the vision were posted there on cards. Another great example is the use of photos to share the story of the vision. A university may set up their common areas with photos of graduates all over the wall, and a medical device company may post pictures of lives they have saved with their devices. Sharing the vision for all to see helps to solidify the meaning in each and every position.

Collaborative Space for a Collaborative Vision

Another way to instill open and constant communication is the configuration of office space or cubicle space. The best visionary leader will place themself in a position that is exposed to the action taking place daily within the organization—gone are the days of the ivory tower and the big glass office. There are more and more examples of CEOs and other high-level executives placing their own offices right in the center of where the team members work.

Further, the designs of today's office configurations are changing. More offices are choosing lower cubicles to allow communication among team members, and many have open floor plans to allow for not only open communication but also employee engagement and understanding of all facets of the business. Within these open floor plans, it is important to have the vision on display for all to see. For example, positive and inspirational messages about teamwork and the power of collaboration in shared spaces will help to develop and support vision. Data charts and graphs that point out prior successes and point to future challenges will support movement towards the goal. These types of visuals can create constant reminders of the vision and the overall objectives of the organization.

Connect the Dots

An exemplary visionary leader will "connect the dots" for the team members, ensuring all team members see their part as a contribution to the whole. This is critical! Team members who understand their contribution to the whole work harder and are more engaged. A leader must help each group and each individual to clarify and understand their contributions to the whole. Recognize and reward team members at all levels of the organization chart and explicitly state how their contributions relate to the overall goal and vision of the organization. This type of exposure clarifies the roles of each person while showing how even a seemingly small act can contribute to the overall success.

Another way a leader can connect the dots is by allowing job-sharing and the crossing of disciplinary lines. This job-sharing technique is used by some of the most innovative and successful organizations. It allows employees to experience other parts of the organization to see how all the parts work together. It clarifies the adage that says you can never truly understand someone until you walk in their shoes.

Back to the sales and marketing aspect of an organization, marketing personnel should spend time in the field with sales team members to physically witness what customers are paying attention to in a product. It also ensures that all employees have time working directly with customers. Yes, even the best exemplary leader should be communicating on a regular basis directly with the consumer—whether that consumer be a child in a K–12 classroom where the principal comes into the classroom on a regular basis to talk to the children, or a user of an end product, the patient in a hospital, or even a university student.

When a leader goes down into the weeds and experiences what the team members do on the front line and, more importantly, what the customer experience is like, the leader is able to better understand how team members live out the vision of the organization to serve the customers. Moreover, when a leader has an authentic conversation with the user of the final end product, they can truly see if the vision of their organization is working at the level of the consumer. If consumers are happy, that means the front line did a good job servicing them and the organization will be more successful.

One university president who was interviewed said she uses numerous engagement opportunities directly with students to connect the dots with the vision. This president participated in a program she called "Pizza with the President." She would pick a dorm or location to set up occasional pizza parties to chat with students in a thoughtful and comfortable environment. She stated it was important these meet-and-greet situations took place in the students' space to increase participation. It was here that she learned so much about students and how to best help them meet their dreams, goals, and aspirations. Students felt respected and empowered by these open conversations and the president felt a better understanding of her customers, the student body.

Another activity this leader participated in to connect the dots with team members was what she called the Magical Mystery Tour. The president wanted to understand the workings of each department within the institution; so to accomplish her mission, she set out to get a tour of each and every department. She went deep into understanding their roles and responsibilities and how each division applied their daily tasks to the overarching vision, mission, and values of the organization. She wanted to experience what her colleagues were experiencing day in and day out. It provided her the clarity she needed on various positions and the tours helped to increase her empathy, understanding, and concern for each group.

Storytelling Successes

As mentioned previously, storytelling is an effective tool to ensure the vision is being communicated. One medical device firm does two things we found successful in sharing the vision. First, on a weekly basis, the team does what they call "The Huddle." The team talks about the important goals for the week and also shares wins in the field. Team members from all areas of the business are involved in the calls, and they are able to share out their successes and challenges. In fact, in one huddle that we listened to, one team member shared a story of how their product saved the life of a young man who was in a motorcycle accident. The life surely would have been lost had they not used the product designed by the team. The hospital previously had not used the product, but for this particular case, it was the only choice they had. They saw the ease of use and, more importantly, that the product stopped the bleeding instantly to allow for all other repairs to the man's broken body to take place. Not surprisingly, the vision for this organization is just that "*No one should bleed to death and the sooner you stop the bleeding, the better.*" By one team member having the opportunity to share this one win, and having this win align and validate the vision, all team members could relate to their value on the team.

Similarly, this same company shares via email success stories and lives saved from the field. Every employee learns of the successes in the field and that the vision is truly met with the use of their product. But the sharing of the vision does not stop there. They share the vision in yet another way: A board is placed in a common area that shows the number of lives saved by their product. When employees pass by this board, they are reminded of the importance of their work. And to take the vision even further, the website visibly displays the number of hospitals and trauma centers that use the product. Finally, the powerful vision is supported by the constant updates on usage for all the customers to see, with the website sharing inspiring stories of the numerous lives saved and the families who benefited from their life-saving technologies. Talk about powerful!

What Keeps Me Up at Night?

We have discussed how leaders can empower followers with the vision, but it is also vital for the leader to feel supported, whether it be by a board of directors, their leaders, or the shareholders. One way for leaders to manage up to the vision is to clearly communicate concerns. Implementing a *What keeps me up at night?* document is a great way for leaders to work with their leadership team on concerns they have regarding the vision or anything critical in the organization. This keeps the line of communication open, both up and down the chain of command. This leads to a "no surprise" policy. Exemplary leaders can also share this document with their team members so that the team knows and understands the leader's concerns.

What keeps me up at night? can range from a simple thought or recent concern to a very detailed explanation of factors that cause overall concerns for the long-term sustainability of the organization. It is here that a leader can show their vulnerability, which oftentimes is not easy for the leader at the top. In fact, one leader in our research stated that being at the top can be a very lonely place. Oftentimes they cannot express their true concerns for fear that it will cause a trickle-down of concerns to the team members. This authentic communication lets everyone know that no one is perfect, we all are human, and we all have fears, dreams, hopes, and aspirations.

To summarize, collaborative visioning is critical to the success of creating a meaning-centered organization. Exemplary leaders who craft the vision with other team members and who then uphold the vision through actions, words, and decision-making will be far more successful than leaders who do not develop a collaborative vision. Building a collaborative vision and rewarding team members for carrying out the vision will transcend into organizational meaning. To assess your behaviors and strategies as they relate to collaborative visioning, please take a moment to answer the Reflection Questions for Collaborative Visioning.

Reflection Questions for Collaborative Visioning

Is our company vision clear and compelling? How can we improve upon it?

Specific ways we developed our vision collaboratively:

Specific ways I uphold the vision through actions, words, and decision-making
  processes throughout the organization:

Is my office in the ivory tower or can I get real and be on the ground floor with the
  troops?

How do we display our vision for all to see?

Chapter 8

Recognition

As a leader your role in enabling and framing meaning is irrefutable.

—Scott Mautz, *Make It Matter*

Recognition and rewards, big and small, are vital to increase empowerment and optimism among team members. Recognition includes inspiration, which can be described as contagious motivation that resonates from the heart. When exemplary leaders recognize and reward their followers, the followers move forward with an increased level of confidence and excitement. This form of enthusiasm and encouragement can create meaning-centered connections and lead to the empowerment people desire.

All of the exemplary leaders in our research mentioned some form of recognition or reward. In our final analysis it was identified as an essential element of their leadership that instills empowerment and optimism. The leaders cited recognition and rewards as a vital tool for communicating accomplishments and reinforcing company values. One leader stated that celebrations were often used to acknowledge expressions of positive character that deserved to be highlighted. The use of recognition to highlight character takes on added importance when you consider that the followers surveyed ranked character as the most important leadership trait. In addition, they scored a leader's ability to recognize the achievements of their teams and individual team members as the number-one way a leader builds inspiration.

You might be surprised by the number of times the leaders in the meaning research described the need to treat others as family. One of the things that most families have in common is the ritual of celebration. From holidays to birthdays and anniversaries, families celebrate. Families also celebrate accomplishments and milestones, such as graduation and promotions.

Making recognition part of the fabric of your organizational family was recommended by the exemplary leaders throughout the research. It is important to celebrate work anniversaries, the births of children, birthdays, and other things that are meaningful to your team members.

The exemplary leaders described company gatherings the way many would describe a family gathering. Holiday gatherings, anniversary parties, and off-site events that provide opportunities to celebrate accomplishments and create the bonds of shared memory were common themes when the leaders responded to how they used the elements of leadership to build a stronger organization. These exemplary leaders understand that their followers need more than a paycheck; they need a sense of belonging—the belonging that deepens with regular opportunities to celebrate and recognize individual and collective efforts.

Several of the leaders described immersing themselves in their work so they would have the opportunity to provide recognition and meet everyone. This notion of connecting with others at their level, or where they work, was also seen as an opportunity to use recognition to inspire, build passion, and ultimately develop empowerment that yields greater work productivity.

There is nothing that says *You Matter* more than a celebration for someone leaving your organization to change to their dream job or to stay home with a new baby. Though we never like to lose a top employee, we must celebrate and recognize the years served. It is okay to have a farewell observation if the situation warrants it and if years of service need to be recognized.

Case in point of lack of celebrations is a situation where employees stated how their organization never even made announcements when two team members left. In fact, both employees were long term and both decided to stay home with new babies. No announcement was made, no celebration of life, no thank you for your service and long-term commitment, no cake, and frankly no recognition. In fact, the company shared nothing with team members until after the team members started spreading the news themselves, through email and on social media. Unfortunately, this lack of communication made others feel "disposable and forgotten." One employee went so far as describing the culture with the words *Sometimes I just feel deleted.* With this lack of recognition, you can understand why an employee would make such a comment.

Leadership theorists and experts agree that recognition is a vital leadership skill. Public recognition of employee effort is built into many of the processes and procedures within a company. Weekly, monthly, or even annual recognition is part of the culture of many organizations; however, these types of performance markers that happen on a scheduled basis, though important, do not go far enough. An employee of the month club or a Friday round-robin is nice, but does not replace the power of nonscripted, unscheduled recognition.

Specific dates and times of recognition and rewards can deplete the effectiveness and authenticity of future recognition.

In fact, leaders today understand the importance of recognition, but oftentimes feel these canned techniques are the solution. And you know it is commonplace when computer applications are being developed to try to make recognition programs automated and easier to implement systemwide. In today's world, you can find applications like Bonusly, Blueboard, Motively, Preciate, and many others. These applications can be downloaded on a computer, as well as a cellphone. Team members can recognize each other in a game-like setting, sharing tokens and distributing awards to teammates for a job well done. These types of applications, like weekly and monthly awards, are wonderful and fun additions to recognition but still cannot replace the spontaneous recognition specifically from a leader to a follower for an on-the-spot job well done.

Leaders need to go beyond the perfunctory measures that provide public accolades. Public praise in the form of recognizing employees with immediate feedback is essential. It lets others know that you are paying attention to their day-to-day efforts. More importantly, it communicates to them that their efforts matter. It is so important to provide different types of recognition, but if you do choose an app, never let the verbal, spontaneous recognition lapse.

Examine the rewards and recognition you currently use in your organization. For recognition to be useful, it must be specific and connected to exemplary performance. We have seen leadership teams discuss monthly awards like they are a slice of the pie to be equally split with all members. When you recognize performance that does not meet standards because it is "someone's turn," it is destructive to morale and culture. Be specific and intentional in how you structure your scheduled rewards and recognition. When people feel recognized, meaning in their work increases.

When a leader exhibits a pattern of recognizing others' work, they are promoting the success of those individuals. Recognition lets others know that their work matters to the success of the organization. It reinforces their value to the mission of the organization and allows for personal meaning from their efforts to grow. Management by walking around (MBWA) is not a new idea, yet leaders often fail to actually use the time to engage and recognize. Consider how many opportunities MBWA can provide for you to appreciate the efforts of your employees. If workers feel they are being ignored, they will feel devalued and their engagement, commitment, and performance will suffer as they lose sight of the meaning of their work.

MBWA will also provide opportunities to spontaneously assess the culture. As you look for positive signs of a strong culture, you will most likely encounter examples where employee behavior does not meet or exceed standards. These are opportunities for leaders to observe and make notes for future corrective strategies to strengthen employees. Save the reprimands for a later time.

The time a leader schedules to practice MBWA is a perfect time for the leader to also hone in on what may be perceived as *small talk*, yet it is hugely important talk. A leader can use these spontaneous, albeit short, conversations to really get to know employees on an authentic level. Having on-the-spot conversations with a few people during this time is critical to walking-the-walk of open communication. It is a time to get to know your employees on a personal basis: *How's the dog? How are the kids? Your wife? Your folks? Did you see the game this weekend?* All of these small conversations can go miles in instilling meaning among team members.

Further, and most important, the leaders can get to know all employee names through the MBWA process! Knowing someone's name is vital to meaning-making. It is shocking to discover that some leaders, even in small businesses, did not know the names of frontline employees, the employees who meet regularly with customers and are the heartbeat of the organization. It may be impossible to learn everyone's name in large organizations, but using the MBWA method certainly will lead to a step in the right direction.

MBWA should include engagement, not only with employees but even with customers. The most senior leader should be engaging in MBWA on a regular basis. Consider the leader who answers the phone or has a conversation with a customer on a regular basis. Imagine the insight, knowledge, and empathy for the employees that the leader can gain through this practice. Understanding the minutia of what makes the organization tick is so vital for a leader to experience. Knowing what the call center does with each customer will add perspective to what is going on in the organization.

Now, there is a very critical note of caution while conducting MBWA! A leader must avoid focusing on a checklist. MBWA is not the time to criticize; it is the time to be casual, be present, stay engaged, and recognize others. It is not a time to worry about corrections; it is a time to have conversations. A young leader Ed worked with years ago quickly became known as a stickler with a clipboard. When conducting walk-throughs, he was notorious for identifying some small shortcomings. His focus on details did not allow him to see the bigger picture of engagement. He was ultimately moved from one site to another until it was determined he would do less damage behind a desk. Sadly, the organization did not intervene with leadership training, and an otherwise bright young leader with loads of potential was sidelined.

Sometimes the forest is more important than the trees. A leader must maintain a 30,000-foot view with the ability to come down to the ground level view when necessity dictates. The biggest mistake this young leader made was constantly looking at the roots of the tree and never at the beauty of the forest. His singular focus was on finding the lack and never the luster. If that is your vantage point, then that is what you will find. Maintaining a mind frame of positive expectation, with a willingness to embrace opportunities for corrective intervention, will enable you to find opportunities for positive reinforcement. In fact, if you have done a thorough job with onboarding and training, you should fully expect to see positive examples of employee effort. And remember, MBWA, like all of the other meaning-centered activities, must be honest, open, and authentic. No one will support it if it is scripted. Everyone can see a fake coming through town.

Awards and public recognition should be especially reserved for those who display effort that is consistent with the ideology of the organization and promotes the culture that is envisioned. Leaders must also pay attention to those who do not display behavior consistent with the organization's vision and culture. Acknowledging lack of effort, or effort that opposes the culture, must also be recognized. Recognizing the lack of effort is better addressed in private, not in public. A leader must ensure that they do not give tacit approval to employees who violate the cultural norms by ignoring incidents that are public.

One of the leaders in our research discussed how they confronted an episode of a violation of a company expectation. A middle manager was observed being overly harsh with a junior employee. By confronting the manager and discussing the issue openly, they got to the core of the issue. The manager admitted to being easily frustrated with managing others. Because this behavior was interrupted, the leader was able to get the manager ongoing leadership coaching. The relationship between the manager and the junior employee was repaired, and the company culture of fairness and treating each other with respect and integrity was upheld.

As mentioned, storytelling is a great way to develop a collaborative vision, but it is also a tool that can be used to recognize others. Several of the leaders described how they used storytelling to inspire employees. They told stories of the company's early days. These stories were about the seemingly heroic growth of the company from an idea to a success. The leaders also told stories about weathering bad economic times. These stories demonstrated the resiliency and grit of the company and its founders. By using these stories during times of recognition and reward, they connected the employees' behavior with the long-term success of the organization and the character traits they hold important.

Examples of how successful companies use recognition are found throughout the business world. Recognition was a repeated theme when Jim Collins and Jerry Porras set out to identify successful habits of visionary companies. From retail to electronics, they found examples of companies that used rewards and recognition to identify employees who exemplified the unique characteristics aligned with the company vision. They described how visionary companies used recognition to promote a tight culture. These companies used both positive and negative reinforcement to establish a "cult-like culture."

Recognition is a vital part of developing the status of the highest performing members of a group. While serving in the Marine Corps, Ed witnessed high-performing Marines receive promotions in public ceremonies. And he also heard about private meetings in the Captain's office where Marines were stripped of rank and demoted. Examples abound of how organizations effectively employ recognition to shape the performance of their members.

Another example of developing meaning is through sharing and publicizing small wins, such as positive comments and reviews from customers, for all to see. Successful leaders allow employees to see the rewards of their efforts and to feel the emotional connection to what they do, which in turn instills meaning in the workplace. To motivate your employees, it is important to provide meaning to what they do. Deep meaning and purpose in the jobs transcends into an employee's personal life. By hearing successes and recognition, such as great reviews from customers, an employee can bring meaning to the work they do. Recognition becomes contagious and the culture experiences both positivity and deep meaning in the products and services they are creating. The positivity transcends throughout the organization by all the leaders who are then able to share this success with the product team members, the R&D department, customer relations, and more.

The culture changes when celebrations are shared and publicly rewarded. Exemplary leaders are skilled at recognizing small wins, which in turn leads to replicated behaviors and bigger wins. Consider the following strategies for success that can be used in your organization to build empowerment through recognition.

STRATEGIES FOR SUCCESS

Using recognition in effective ways allows for a leader to promote expectations and shape the culture of the organization. By keeping recognition at the forefront of your leadership, you can deepen your impact. Below we outline some of the common tips and strategies to recognize and reward team members through inspiration. Remember, it is vital the leadership team be spontaneous and authentic with rewards and recognition. Meaning is created when employees realize their daily efforts matter. When an exemplary leader remembers to call out the wins—both big and small—meaning is created!

Respect and Appreciation

One simple way for a leader to support the efforts of others is communicating respect. Does everyone on your team get handshakes or high-fives; or do you reserve respect and appreciation for a select few favorites on your team?

Perhaps only your top performers? A leader can grow empowerment through the simple act of recognizing others with respect and appreciation. The aloof leader, who is too preoccupied to acknowledge his or her staff regardless of their position, will diminish empowerment with every perceived slight.

A leader must also ensure they take time to remind others of the importance of their efforts. This personal acknowledgment can deepen commitment, strengthen a collective sense of belonging, and help to create meaning. An exceptional superintendent ended each meeting with a reminder of how valuable each person's contributions were to the organization. As he described this impact, he clarified values of importance. "Your hard work and deep commitment is appreciated. Without your efforts our organization would not be where it is today."

Under ten years of this type of leadership, there was very little turnover within the management team; more importantly, test scores rose every year for each of those ten years. The combined hard work and commitment the superintendent recognized in his meetings was predictive of the behavior of this team. During site visits he acknowledged everyone he encountered. Handshakes and high-fives were shared in abundance. The respect and appreciation of each employee's efforts was clear. Appreciation is a simple act of human kindness that is often overlooked in the workplace, yet resonates positivity and builds a meaningful culture.

Stay Present

In order to observe positive examples of company expectations, you must engage workers where they are and stay present. This takes MBWA one level deeper. That means coming out of your office and conducting regular walk-throughs. This will provide you the opportunity to spontaneously use positive reinforcement. With regular MBWA moments, you can stay current with what is happening at the core of the organization.

While walking around, it is a good time to make note of changes in behaviors, attitudes, and culture. By staying present, you will be better able to assess the overall health of the organization. It is too easy to sit in your ivory tower and ignore what is happening on the front line, which can be fatal. By being present, you will be more apt to notice small changes to attitudes or behaviors within the organizational culture. When changes are noticed, you can address them head-on. If you do not stay present, engagement can erode rapidly. Walk-throughs can also be followed up with a brief note, email, or personal message.

One university president explained that his regular example of staying present took place on accounts payable days. Instead of using interoffice mail to deliver checks back to the payables department, he hand-delivered the

checks after signing them. He emphasized that, since the accounting department was on the other side of the building, this allowed him weekly engagement with numerous employees along the way. He would wander past desks,
noticing the small things, like a new picture in the office or bouquet of flowers
on a desk. He would take these moments to engage on a personal level.

Another great example was the leader who explained her *Magical Mystery
Tour*. She would set her sights on visiting each department to engage with
others, stay up to date with new happenings, and make note of recognition
opportunities. These *tours*, she said, helped her to touch base with all departments to feel the pulse of the organization and to be sure it was functioning
as it should be.

"Wow" Cards

Throughout the research on *Meaning-Centered Leadership*, we found numerous ways in which to share wins, including acts such as producing something
like "Wow" or "Way to Go" cards, which can be emailed to team members
for a job well done. This is different from handwritten notes of appreciation. This is an electronic note or graphic that specifically addresses a *wow*
moment in the workplace. Perhaps someone just landed a big account or a
customer sent a rave review. It is typically very quick, very spontaneous, and
very short. Of course, this is in addition to verbal celebrations publicly as you
just wander around.

By publicly recognizing others, leaders instill a sense of pride with employees. Positive influence from a leader is demonstrated through being present;
communicating effectively and often with all employees, rewarding, recognizing, and celebrating small wins; and leading by example. Wow cards are just one
more simple tool that can be implemented immediately and with no hard costs.

Barbara personally used Wow and way-to-go cards in an electronic format
for a dispersed team model. The recognition cards can be created in a simple
software application like PowerPoint or Publisher. When she heard of an
accomplishment, big or small, from a team member or colleague, she updated
the little electronic card with the recipient's photo and a small description of
the success. This card was then emailed to her two main departments in celebration of the win. Team members throughout the state were able to enjoy
the wins of others. Also, by sharing photos in the electronic Wow card, team
members in the dispersed model were able to attach a face to the name.

Meaning is created, successes are celebrated, and the team members work
harder because they know their work matters! This practice is so simple, yet
so appreciated. Further, others in the organization can replicate the idea and
send similar items out on their own. A positive culture is contagious! Wow
cards can recognize anyone in the organization and, if it comes from top

leadership, imagine how it will make the entire team feel! Authentic recognition at its finest!

Team Shopping Days

One of the most exciting reward days Barbara experienced with her team was a shopping day. One afternoon, during a training and development week, the day culminated in a very engaging scavenger hunt. Team members were broken into small groups and were given numerous activities to solve, while learning more about the university. At the end of the scavenger hunt, the team ended up at the university bookstore. Team members were rewarded with a university shopping spree, with a set dollar amount to spend. The excitement level was high. Smiles and celebrations ensued. Everyone got exactly what they wanted, from selfie-sticks to sweatshirts.

This small celebratory moment was appreciated by every employee. The team was reminded of this special moment each time they enjoyed their new find. Both the scavenger hunt and the shopping spree allowed for personal conversations between employees. Relationships strengthened and positivity increased.

Celebration Days

Another great way to reward and recognize others is to celebrate their special days with potluck lunches or a cake to share. Who would not want to celebrate a birthday or work anniversary? People love to feel celebrated, especially on their birthday. If the organization is large, you can have one day set aside to recognize everyone at the same time who is celebrating a birthday or work anniversary that month. If the organization is small, you can have the celebrations independently, or by department.

Starting these special days off right would also include a company-wide email to celebrate those names in writing. This is effective if implemented from the top down, with the support of human resources. Celebrations like this let team members know they matter. Employees give so much of their time and energy to their work, a simple "thank you for time" served can reap exponential rewards through engagement. Further, these small gatherings allow time for team members to engage with each other on a personal level, improving relationships among team members.

Notes of Appreciation

We discussed handwritten notes of appreciation extensively in chapter 5, but it is important to note that these small acts of appreciation are effective when

discussing recognition, as well. Make a habit of sending notes of appreciation to team members. This serves a few purposes. First, it reinforces that you
care for your employees and helps to build the caring undercurrent needed for
meaning to flourish. Second, it allows you to express elements of the core ideology of the company. Finally, these expressions of gratitude serve to deepen
the leaders' commitment and satisfaction to others. Multiple researchers and
psychologists have described the role that gratitude plays in deepening well-
being. Reinforcing your own well-being while creating meaning for your
followers is a win-win.

In summary, recognition, much like care and concern, can make a big
difference in how you are perceived by your followers. People like to be recognized for a job well done. In addition, this recognition can build the much-
needed self-esteem in individuals so they can move up to the highest level
of self-actualization. Humans want to feel needed and valued. To assess your
behaviors and strategies as they relate to recognition, please take a moment to
answer the Reflection Questions related to Recognition. Be mindful of ways
to recognize and reward others for a job well done.

In the next chapter we look at the leader's role in establishing a deep
day-to-day pattern of enthusiastically approaching their work. As you read
through the next chapter, you will see the need for leaders to focus on their
own commitment, workplace satisfaction, and well-being. You must possess
these skills in high degrees to ensure you are that rare breed of leader who
never has a bad day.

Reflection Questions for Recognition

When was the last time I actually practiced MBWA, and what did I learn from it?

When did the other key leaders in my organization practice authentic MBWA?

The last time I spoke directly with an end-user/customer was:

The last time I had authentic conversations with my direct reports about their goals
  and aspirations, I learned:

How many Wow cards and notes of appreciation have I sent, and why?

Chapter 9

Enthusiasm

> Success consists of going from failure to failure without loss of enthusiasm.

> —Winston Churchill

Empowerment is cemented when others are entrusted to enthusiastically pursue work that connects to their strengths. Leading with enthusiasm can motivate and inspire the team to move forward. The foundation for organizational enthusiasm begins with trust, as we have discussed extensively. When a leader builds engagement and establishes trustworthiness, they create an environment where passion and enthusiasm can flourish. A leader who has taken the time to know the strengths of their employees, and capitalizes on these strengths, will be in position to create a dynamic and enthusiastic workplace.

One of the important traits a leader must possess is the ability to bring high levels of day-to-day enthusiasm to their work. Research identified several ways that leaders build enthusiasm, including bringing a positive attitude to the workplace. Exemplary leaders concurred that enthusiasm and passion are critically important to creating inspiration and meaning within an organization.

Research participants agreed that a leader must be able to express their enthusiasm. One leader summed up the importance of enthusiasm when he stated, "You've got to be able to get people excited! A leader needs to be a cheerleader." Further, in describing a difficult situation, he decided he needed to encourage his/her team with enthusiasm. He said, "I need to give a pep talk . . . these are our challenges and this is what we need to do . . . and we can do it!" It is vital that a leader keep his team encouraged and energized, especially during times of change and challenges. To do so, a leader must empower team members through enthusiasm.

In total, our research participants placed the need to enthusiastically inspire their followers as one of most important elements of their leadership. They explained that the day-to-day implementation of the vision needs to be actionable. Their daily enthusiasm can guide the implementation of the vision and provide important touch points for meaning to be created.

The need to embrace challenges in an upbeat and positive manner was another area of agreement among the exemplary leaders. One leader stated that finding a positive angle to each and every problem was essential. Finding positivity in a stack of concerns can make the situation more bearable. Moreover, working from a place of positivity with an expectation for a positive outcome is essential. In effect, a positive approach was a bottom-line expectation for this leader.

Another exemplary leader described enthusiasm coming from the process of followers owning the vision. When others see themselves within the vision and the efforts of the organization, they become empowered, passionate, and enthusiastic about their work. This process was seen by the leader as an essential aspect of their leadership. They described the need to capture the passion of their followers.

One clear fact was identified by the research: the leaders were in agreement that keeping others inspired and deeply engaged is the responsibility of leaders. The leaders described a variety of ways to achieve an impassioned team, from creating expectations for a positive culture to focusing on future outcomes. Exemplary leaders found a variety of ways to deliver on this essential role of being a leader who creates meaning.

Research contends that a leader can inspire passion in team members, which validates excitement and the ability to share ideas with other team members. As one author noted, "Through their magnetism and quiet persuasion, leaders enlist others in their dreams. They breathe life into their visions and get people to see exciting possibilities for the future."[1] Further, Kouzes and Posner put it succinctly when they said, "The best leaders are the most passionate about their work, their organizations, and their disciplines. Their enthusiasm is contagious, and others catch that enthusiasm and display it in their own work."[2] Enthusiasm certainly is contagious and can build team members up and get them excited for the vision and mission of the workplace.

According to Robert Greenleaf, author of *Servant Leadership*, the leaders in today's organizations must be able to conceptualize a more holistic institution that can encourage others to be enthusiastic about being a part of the larger organization. Leaders must lead with this meaningful goal in mind. Let others enthusiastically know they are part of a bigger whole. Become the organization that people want to work for! Today it is not just about the pay-check. There is a new method in today's workforce to becoming the preferred organization.

Employees today will demand that organizations see beyond the exchange of money for labor. "The next step may be to acknowledge that every person is entitled to work that is meaningful in individual terms."[3] Greenleaf made these comments in 2002 and yet today meaning still is not a focus of leader-ship. Today, more than ever, meaning matters. The workforce of the twenty-first century will continue to demand it. Today's workplace demands must be more about working for an organization that supports meaning and purpose, which in turn will increase employee engagement, fulfillment, and happiness. Ultimately, by shifting the focus of the American workplace, productivity and profitability will rise.

Enthusiasm builds inspiration, which can lead to empowerment and posi-tivity. As mentioned, enthusiasm and positivity are contagious and can per-meate throughout the organization if the leader keeps them at the forefront of importance. Experiences that are positive, hopeful, and loving provide meaning in the long run for both leaders and followers.

In addition to enthusiasm, building positivity and inspiration allows employees to take risks and empowers them to take the lead of projects. Leadership studies focused on transformational leadership have identified inspirational leadership as the ability to help others become motivated beyond self-interest. It is in this space beyond self-interest that true meaning can be created. When you serve your employees in ways that promote their well-being, you will demonstrate an approach that focuses on others and not your own self-interest.

Early in Ed's career in school leadership, he heard an award-winning prin-cipal associate her success with the fact that she did not believe she could have a bad day. She believed her enthusiasm for each moment of each day was needed to keep others passionately engaged in the important task of edu-cating children. Similarly, enthusiastic leadership has been associated with creating an atmosphere that promotes high performance and is conducive to innovation.

The consistent behavior of the leader to communicate to their followers their true intentions is imperative. Your actions must match your words. Just like the principal who believed she could not have a bad day, your enthusi-asm should be on display on a regular basis. The employees in your orga-nization take their cues from you, and they are always watching. When you enter a room enthusiastically, the vibe in the room becomes contagious and enthusiasm prevails. Conversely, if you enter a room frustrated or angry, the air in the room will be heavier and the mood of the attendees will immedi-ately begin to mimic your presence. This is easy to test out: try it sometime and see how the room reacts to different entries. Modeled behaviors are important.

Enthusiasm is especially important when assisting others in implementing complex ideas or managing change initiatives. Deep meaning can be found in enthusiastic engagement in challenging tasks. A leader creates an opportunity for employees to connect with deep meaning by creating opportunities to work on tasks that match their skill set, that challenges their skillset, and on matters of deep organizational importance. Giving employees the autonomy to work in this fashion will allow them to bring enthusiasm to their tasks.

The inspiration that comes from daily enthusiasm can be described as the ability to have others follow with enthusiasm, hope, and optimism. Strong leaders will look at obstacles or weaknesses as opportunities. The enthusiastic leader will convey messages of positivity through difficult times, encouraging team members to watch for the bright side when a change is fully implemented, for example. The positive leader will always find the silver lining and will share their enthusiasm with others. A positive attitude and a positive outlook are critical traits for a strong leader, as are reliability and resiliency. Through these relationships, team members have the freedom to share ideas, techniques, and enthusiasms, which in turn can drive the passion further and raise the bar on personal and professional achievements. By building enthusiasm, an exemplary leader can light the fire for others.

As previously stated, the work environment of today requires a new type of leadership. The leadership focus today must be on creating an environment conducive to building meaning. For leaders to maintain this outlook, it is essential that they focus on the key elements of leadership as laid out in this book. Enthusiasm must be a genuine expression of a leaders' desire to create transformative experiences for their employees. There are numerous strategies that can help leaders build enthusiasm within their teams.

STRATEGIES FOR SUCCESS

Below you will find tried-and-true strategies to support the implementation and sustainment of enthusiasm. An enthusiastic leader is not just a cheerleader but is there to support team members through good times and difficult times. Enthusiasm must be genuine and authentic. It is not just a rah-rah moment but true positivity and support for the team. Empowerment is strengthened when a leader builds enthusiasm and positivity in the workplace. Fortunately, there are several things a leader can do to maintain a feeling of genuine enthusiasm in their leadership. Outlined below are some behaviors and strategies to help build an enthusiastic culture within organizations. By implementing some of these tips and strategies, you will be on your way to becoming a meaning-centered leader.

Mindset to Serve Others

Enthusiasm begins with mindset. A leader must understand that leadership is a privilege that carries enormous responsibilities. A leader's most important role is serving others. Martin Luther King, Jr., said we can all be great because we can all serve. Exemplary leaders understand that they serve others, just as their team members serve others for the benefit of the organization.

Maintaining a focus on how your leadership serves the needs of others is essential to maintaining a high degree of enthusiasm. Great inspiration and enthusiasm should be drawn from the opportunity to serve others through your leadership. By serving your employees in ways that build meaning and enhance their well-being, you will simultaneously build their capacity to be productive members of your organization. By serving them, you serve your organization and strengthen your leadership. Great enthusiasm should be drawn from the potential impact of servant leadership.

Staying focused on the needs of others as well as maintaining your enthusiasm is not necessarily a natural or easy task. A leader can most certainly take steps to ensure they are focusing their energies in ways that maximize their impact. And this mindset to serve others can come through the smallest acts of assistance, from holding the door open for someone with their hands full to taking on a task that someone else just does not have the time to handle. Opportunities for service to others can be found daily if you keep your eyes and ears open to it.

One small act of kindness witnessed in an organization was from an administrative assistant to the chief operating officer (COO) of a very large, nationwide radio station. The assistant to the COO would occasionally go out unprompted to get a much-needed coffee for her boss. Now some might think, well that's her job, which it is not, but is more of an act of kindness. The assistant goes one step further in her kindness. Each time the coffee shows up, a small heart is drawn on the lid! This heart just brightens the day of the COO. As mentioned, some exemplary leaders expressed that it could be quite lonely at the top due to additional burdens required of senior management, but this act of kindness from one person can make a challenging day a bit more bearable. The heart could be seen with each sip of coffee and the COO knew she was loved and that she had a great team supporting her.

An Attitude of Gratitude

Expressions of gratitude to those you serve will help you to focus on creating an enthusiastic workplace. Earlier in the book we discussed positive recognition for your employees. By accentuating positives and focusing on employee skills that build their productivity, you will naturally demonstrate more positive enthusiasm. Avoiding a deficit mindset is essential. The young clipboard leader who was mentioned in chapter 8 was plagued by deficit thinking. He mistakenly thought his role was to fastidiously identify everyone's faults so they could be rectified. Instead, he created a dispirited work environment marked by deep employee resentment. His interactions became defensive because of the pushback he constantly received from employees. As that defensiveness grew, his leadership was doomed.

An attitude of gratitude, similar to a servant leadership mindset, can happen regularly when one focuses on seeking opportunities for gratitude. Recognize and appreciate others through regular words and comments like *please*, *thank you*, *great job*, and *you rock!* Just short comments and small acts of kindness, to friends and strangers alike, can go a long way to inspiring a mindset of gratitude.

It is critical that leaders do not just talk the talk of gratitude. Exemplary leaders actually practice what they preach and they practice it openly for others to see and model. The best leaders also encourage other team members to do the same—creating a contagious culture of gratitude. When everyone lives their lives with a gratitude mindset, the culture breeds positivity and engagement. When colleagues thank and appreciate each other, the whole environment improves and meaningfulness is formed. We challenge you to express gratitude numerous times per day. Watch how it not only builds enthusiasm in the recipients but also brightens your own spirits. It just feels good to appreciate others and to be appreciated.

Strength-Based Environment

Creating a strength-based environment takes intentionality. You will see areas that need improvement, but how you address opportunities for growth is crucial. If you have taken the time to build trusting relationships, your attempts at improving performance will be received much more constructively. If you have taken the time to acknowledge strengths, others will notice.

A strengths-based approach to leadership has been written about extensively. Numerous authors have discussed how to find your own strengths, as well as how to support the strengths of your employees, so all team members are working more effectively toward a common goal. One best-selling book on strengths-based leadership is by Tom Rath, based on Dr. Donald Clifton's research, entitled *StrengthsFinder 2.0*. Dr. Clifton is known to have led over 10 million people to seek out their strengths and use them to capitalize on meaningful and purposeful work. As the studies by Gallup and Dr. Clifton have found, people who focus on their given strengths and abilities are six times more likely to have higher engagement levels in the workplace. Further, people who learn how to work in partnership with their strengths have expressed a better quality of life overall than their counterparts who do not.

A strengths-based approach of coaching does take effort on the part of the leader. To lead someone to capitalize on their strengths, a leader must become a coach and an accountability partner. It requires the ability to have open and honest conversations with employees to assess their long-term goals and aspirations. It takes asking your team members: *Where do you want to be in three years, five years, ten years?* The leader must have the confidence to coach, knowing that they may be coaching out one of their finest employees! A leader must ask questions such as: *What do you like about your job? What do you dislike? What would you like to see different? How can I help you do more of what you love?* Talking to your employees about their passions and their future allows you an opportunity to build a connection with their future. Ongoing training and professional development must be applied at the individual level to ensure commitment, continuity, and connection to the goals and aspirations of each team member.

Most importantly, a leader should not ask these questions if they are not willing to follow through on the development of team member through growth and other opportunities, even if it means leaving their department. There is nothing more depleting to an employee than a leader who asks a question but does not follow through or follow up on the promise to help a team member get to the next level.

If you, as a leader, do not have the power to help the person grow to their most desired position, make that clear in the conversation. Be honest in letting the person know you are willing to help develop their goals and desires, but that you are not in the position of power to provide a position they are seeking. Allow them the opportunities to continue to develop toward their ultimate goal, and encourage them to apply for positions as they become available, but do not promise anything that cannot be delivered, as an empty promise can break trust and diminish the employee's overall commitment to the leader.

There are numerous examples of overpromising, but underdelivering, intentional or not, in organizations. One employee shared the story that she wanted to move into a training and development role. The leader falsely implied through immediate actions and words that such opportunities were in abundance. The employee stated that four years later, not only did the opportunity never come to fruition, but she witnessed the same leader offering a new employee the exact same opportunity. In fact, the longer-term employee was then offered the chance to be on a team with the newest employee to develop training materials!. It was as if the promise was completely forgotten.

The first employee saw the cycle of empty promises being replicated right in front of her very eyes. The employee was furious, not only that the promises of years past were never brought to fruition but even more so that a new employee was given the same carrot to chew. She wanted to forewarn the new employee that she was given the same promise years earlier, but the goals fell into the wind. Trust was broken. The long-term employee was shattered, and the new employee was unknowingly being duped.

The leader failed in the leadership role to follow through and follow up with appropriate coaching and opportunities to develop a motivated employee. The leader failed by breaking trust and lying to the new employee, unbeknownst to her, yet loud and clear to the others. Trust was diminished throughout the division as a result of the long-term employees recognizing that promises were broken. Further, the employees shared their frustrations, which contributed to lower motivation for others. Trust and culture were negatively impacted.

Emotional Intelligence

A leader must also focus on maintaining their own emotional regulation. The right mindset must be matched by the right emotional reaction to issues impacting your workplace. An enthusiastic leader is an emotionally predictable leader. A single episode of an emotional outburst could potentially create irreparable harm.

A dramatic case in point developed when researching the cause of a director's dismissal. Somewhere between the press clippings and the director's public statements, the truth could be found. A staff member spoke of how he entered her office one day, slammed the door blocking her exit, and then berated her for showing disrespect in a meeting. It turns out his first mistake was thinking he could demand respect, the second was misinterpreting a situation, but the biggest mistake was the director's actions. The female staff member had endured a long and abusive relationship before breaking free.

You can imagine the immediate flashback of this type of angry and aggressive confrontation that she experienced. Worse for this leader was the fact that this story quickly made the rounds of the staff members who supported her through the difficulties of the abuse she endured. This leader did not listen, and he did not value the opinions of his staff. His meetings were silent, and his relationships withered with every angry outburst. The truth is, he resigned due to pressure put on the board by the very people he was supposed to serve.

A leader must have the ability to manage the complex array of emotions that encompass human experience. A leader should strive to be the calm in the storm with regard to expressing negative emotions. If they are misinterpreted as aggression, as was the case with the director from the above scenario, you will be viewed as a bully and your credibility will be shot.

In summary, an enthusiastic leader has several tools at their disposal to ensure they maintain their enthusiasm. First, start with a mindset of serving others. That mindset will allow you to focus on building the capabilities of others. Second, express gratitude to those you lead. These expressions of gratitude will build their enthusiasm and keep your fires of enthusiasm constantly stoked. This approach will also allow you to build a strength-based environment. Finally, maintain an emotional regulation that allows you to respond to challenges as opportunities to help others grow. If your employees begin to question your emotional reaction to challenges, they will begin to question their own responses, and nothing constructive will take place. However, if you serve your employees with gratitude, while focusing on their strengths and managing your own emotions, you will build an enthusiastic environment that allows for deep personal meaning to be created.

Again, take some time to evaluate your leadership skills by answering the Reflection Questions for Enthusiasm. Determine how many of the success strategies are used to create enthusiasm and how you can improve upon building this important element to achieve a meaning-centered approach.

Reflection Questions for Enthusiasm

The last time I had to practice my emotional intelligence was:

The most effective strategy for me in practicing an attitude of gratitude is:

The ways in which I implement strength-based leadership so employees can have opportunities to establish meaning include:

A scenario where I last experienced and practiced servant-leadership was:

SUMMARY OF EMPOWERMENT

In Part II, we provided a framework for the importance of collaborative visioning, recognition, and enthusiasm for building empowerment among your employees. We described the need for developing and always working toward a vision that was developed collaboratively. Empowering your employees through recognition and enthusiasm will provide the opportunity for meaning and purpose to develop. With empowerment, your team will experience high levels of satisfaction in the work they do every day. Empowerment increases engagement, and again the 3Es of *Meaning-Centered Leadership* are intertwined.

In Part III we will discuss expertise and how leaders can share their expertise through wisdom and humility. Further, we will discuss the third element of expertise and how a meaning-centered leader provides team members an opportunity for an optimistic future.

Part III

EXPERTISE

The best executive is the one who has sense enough to pick good men to do what he wants done, and self-restraint enough to keep from meddling with them while they do it.

—Theodore Roosevelt

Elements of Expertise.

Expertise is the third E in the 3Es that creates the *Meaning-Centered Leadership* approach. Expertise contains three elements which allow for meaning to be created. The first element is wisdom based on exemplary character traits. Wisdom is strengthened when a leader's character is one of upmost honesty and integrity.

The second element of expertise is optimism, confidently leading teams to an optimistic future. The nature of the modern workplace demands leaders who can lead through innovation and change. Teams of inspired people working toward an optimistic future are required to generate the constant innovation necessary to remain competitive in a fast-paced and ever-changing society. Leaders must have deep expertise in order to lead their teams towards a future that may not yet exist, while keeping the reality of today in focus.

The last of the three elements in expertise is practicing humility as a leader. The ability for a leader to be humble, to recognize the efforts of others before self, is vital to becoming a meaning-centered leader. There is no room for arrogance or narcissism in the *Meaning-Centered Leadership* approach.

Before beginning the section on expertise, take a moment to jot down your thoughts on the Reflection Questions for Expertise. Think about how you display wisdom, optimism, and humility as a leader.

Reflection Questions for Expertise

Ways I demonstrate wisdom include:

Specific ways I express optimism for the future include:

Specific reasons why I believe I am a humble leader include:

Specific examples of expressing humility include:

As we are all well aware, many of the jobs of today will not exist in the years to come. Jobs will continue to be eliminated as new technologies, such as artificial intelligence and robotics, are developed. Organizations will continue to evolve, be eliminated, or change as the new technological advancements are implemented. Consider the video stores and bookstores of just a few short years ago. Stores such as Blockbuster had to change with the times, through VCRs and DVDs. Today, with the advent of streaming services, these stores are obsolete.

In addition to jobs being eliminated, new jobs will be created. In fact, a 2017 report published by the Institute for the Future and by Dell Technologies says that 85 percent of the jobs that will be available in 2030 have not even been invented yet![1] This is only one short decade away. We have to educate our children of today for jobs we do not even know about for tomorrow. It will take great leaders to lead this force, and continual professional development will be a must. We do not have all the answers as to what the future holds for jobs in the decades to come, but we do know that leadership will continue to be the most important aspect of employee engagement and organizational success.

Furthermore, the Institute for the Future discusses how jobs will be seeking top employees from all over the world, and technology will allow leaders to match experts with desired skills. People will go to jobs that align with their passion and expertise to create greater happiness and meaning in their lives. This is where a meaning-centered leader will add value to the organization. A meaning-centered leader will use their skills and expertise to match their employees to the desired path, creating a happier employee, a happier customer base, and a more profitable organization.

Today's leaders are challenged to create organizational meaning and clarity regardless of, or in spite of, difficult circumstances. In fact, difficult times create opportunities for leaders to build organizational meaning for themselves and others. Consider Viktor Frankl's concentration camp epiphany: "We should not then, be hesitant about challenging man with a potential meaning for him to fulfill. It is only thus that we evoke his will to meaning from its state of latency."[2]

In these challenging times, leaders must rely on the knowledge they have gained and the principles that guide their work. They must be able to guide their followers through challenges by focusing on principles and maintaining a wildly optimistic view for the future. Passion cannot be programmed, yet the passion to apply oneself can be inspired by the leader who has honed in on their soft skills of empathy, humility, creativity, and wisdom.

Part III focuses on the leader's role in using their wisdom gained by experience and informed by their principles. Research shows that followers expect leaders to bring the knowledge of personal experience to bear on the challenges of the organization. Followers also expect leaders to keep the goals of the organization continuously at the forefront. These two leadership behaviors are how a leader can express wisdom. The steady march of knowledge based on experience, informed by organizational principles and goals, allows leaders to build a strong organizational culture, a culture built on high expectation and commitment to creating a better future from today's work.

When I think back to my first leadership opportunity after serving in the United States Marine Corps., I am reminded of how leadership uninformed by principles, optimism, and humility can fail. By equal parts hard work, serendipity, and circumstance, I found myself leading a large dynamic organization at the ripe old age of twenty-two. As a recently separated Marine, I was still adjusting to civilian life. I was used to being surrounded by hundreds of people that dressed like me, talked like me, and believed, as I did, that we were lean mean fighting machines. Needless to say, that young arrogant man had neither the wisdom nor the humility to rise to the challenges of the leadership in front of him. Regardless of age and experience, the expertise we express in this part of the book must be grounded in universal principles.

Principles I lost sight of all those years ago while trying to fill a role that out-sized my preparation. We hope you find in Part III the opportunity to reflect on the values by which an exemplary leader should live and lead.

In the book *Built to Last*, Collins and Porras stated that highly successful organizations contain visionary leaders who articulate a vision that supports a core ideology and stimulates progress toward a new future. As mentioned previously, a shared vision with clear lines of communication and alignment of goals and values will lead to success. The vision supports the expertise of the leadership team and sets the foundation for what the organization can become. Leaders get team members on board to reach the dreams and goals of the organization through wisdom, optimism for the future, and sharing of expertise while practicing humility. Let's continue the journey to understand the elements of expertise: wisdom, optimism, and humility.

Chapter 10

Wisdom

> True wisdom comes to each of us when we realize how little we
> understand about life, ourselves, and the world.
>
> —Socrates

Wisdom is using one's past knowledge and experiences grounded by principles and values to make decisions about future situations. Wisdom provides insights and understanding into organizational behaviors and performance. Wisdom goes much deeper than just having knowledge or expertise about a particular subject. Wisdom is critically dependent on ethics, judgment, insight, creativity, and other transcendent forms of human intellection. Wisdom is less about what one knows and more about how one behaves and acts in sharing their knowledge.

Followers expect their leaders to be experts in their fields. Expertise, accompanied by clear guiding principles and consistency, helps to build culture and creates important meaning-making inputs. The wisdom of a leader builds confidence and trust for followers within the organization.

Followers want an exemplary leader to instill their personal wisdom within the organization. Employees benefit from hearing the experiences and stories from their leaders to validate the successes from past situations. By sharing the knowledge and wisdom learned from previous experiences, leaders can pave the way to creating meaning in the organization. Behaviors related to wisdom include bringing past experiences to a situation, using storytelling to compare future and past scenarios, and displaying expertise and understanding.

The exemplary leaders in the research all described organizational wisdom as a crucial element of their leadership. Interestingly, the leaders had divergent ways to promote organizational wisdom. One leader cited the need to create a strong organizational culture carefully aligned to core values. Another leader suggested that organizational wisdom was created by team problem-solving in a transparent environment. Mentoring was cited by one leader as the way organizational wisdom grows.

The varied descriptions by these leaders point out the fact that there are several ways in which leaders can ensure they focus on building organizational wisdom. It is also interesting to note that all the leaders agreed that sound business principles, processes, and procedures are the required elements for building organizational wisdom. As one leader put it, "Without sound business processes you won't have an organization." The leaders were in agreement that sound processes allow for problem solving that leads to organizational wisdom. They also described wisdom as being a derivative of experience and felt mentoring was a way to develop organizational wisdom.

The exemplary leaders clearly viewed organizational wisdom as comprising the ability of their teams to solve complex problems. However, the followers surveyed clearly identified that they expect their leader to bring personal wisdom to their work while keeping the goals of the organization at the forefront of their conversations. The idea that organizational wisdom is shared is consistent with additional findings in the literature and is also consistent with an engaged and empowered workplace. The fact that followers expect wisdom from their leaders should come as no surprise.

Interestingly, exemplary leaders also expect wisdom from their team members. Several of the leaders stated they cannot always be the smartest person in the room. Others mentioned they looked for answers from others. This expression of collective wisdom is not new. The leaders explained that wisdom is often expressed by knowing what you do not know and being okay with expressing that. Avoiding the notion that your title makes you the smartest in the room was another idea expressed by the leaders.

Expressing with clarity where the company is going and how it will get there is most certainly a consistent theme when the exemplary leaders discuss wisdom. Often the earlier elements of leadership within the engagement and empowerment framework come together when discussing wisdom. It is clear the leaders shared a common theme that having a culture built on a solid foundation of ethical behavior is required to have a wise organization.

Perhaps more importantly, the leaders voiced an understanding that the wisdom must be attained from the collective. If wisdom is to guide the group, it only makes sense that wisdom is derived from the group. Leadership must engage and empower others through conversations that ask questions and establish that there is an expectation for shared creation of elements of the company vision. A vision that expresses the wisdom of the organization is truly built by the collective team. Further, a collective vision is much more likely to be successful at guiding day-to-day actions within the organization.

Research shows a clear link between leadership and wisdom. Leaders who can share their wisdom with followers are able to build personal and organizational meaning. Researchers agree that leaders use wisdom to engage, inspire, and motivate followers. In short, exemplary leaders use wisdom to build organizational meaning by creating and communicating the important values of the organization.

One must create a strong culture with careful alignment to core values if you hope to have a wise organization. One way to ensure that alignment is to write a core values statement. Your core values should be clear and actionable to guide behavior. They should indicate the behavior required to achieve the mission of the organization. For example, integrity, professionalism, growth-mindset, and self-regulation are all core values that can be illustrated through actions and described via examples.

By collaboratively developing the core values of the organization, a leader can demonstrate their wisdom. When developing the core values, it is vital to ensure that inputs from all employees, at all levels, are represented. More importantly, the core values must be shared and practiced by all, from the CEO to the janitor, the C-Suite to the call center. It is imperative that the core values are referenced often so that all team members know and understand their importance to the overall organizational mission.

It is one thing to have written core values; it is another to ensure they are followed. A wise leader will reward value alignment on a regular basis and, more importantly, reprimand misalignment quickly and severely. By practicing core values and assessing the alignment of the core values, leaders can ensure consistency in behaviors throughout the organization.

Misalignment to the core values is sadly becoming more commonplace. Just consider the numerous allegations that have been brought to the forefront of many organizations today! We see examples on the news daily. The perceived wisdom of a leadership team can be utterly diminished when top leaders do not dismiss employees for core value misalignment. For example, if an organization has a top leader who is considered a bully by team members, yet leadership loves him because he is intelligent and good at his job, leadership really needs to consider the consequences of not letting this leader go. If the team members are miserable, afraid, beat-up, dejected, and diminished, imagine what those feelings are doing to the team's engagement levels. More importantly, consider what is happening to the culture, the productivity levels, and, ultimately, the bottom line.

If the stated core values of an organization include words like *integrity, trust, collaboration, teamwork,* and *honesty,* yet a team leader is able to get away with being short-tempered, abusive, and not able to have a true open-door policy through active listening with open communication, then the team will suffer. Such leaders tend to use their power to manipulate people in their department, yet they are skilled at managing up to their own leadership. This is the reason all leaders at all levels must use their wisdom to assess their team leaders. Ensure core values of all members are in alignment and that each and every employee's behaviors match the values desired. Monitor employee assessments often to ensure what you believe to be true is accurate from the employee perspective.

> "Wisdom lies not in what is known but rather in the manner in which knowledge is held and in how that knowledge is put to use."
>
> John Meacham

Exemplary leaders can put the wisdom gained throughout their leadership journey to use in their organization to create meaning. Martin Seligman described a variety of individual character traits that demonstrate wisdom, including curiosity, love of learning, open-mindedness, creativity, and perspective.

Wisdom develops in leaders through life experiences, empathy, and emotional maturity. A combination of the exemplary leader's character traits and experiential learning impacts the wisdom and knowledge a leader brings into the workplace. Wisdom is acquired from what one has learned in different life phases, yet wisdom is developed in individuals at different levels. Wisdom is oftentimes termed as a sixth sense, which allows a wise leader to effectively plan, manage, and evaluate situations while supporting and giving feedback to followers.

Some researchers theorize that the way to develop wisdom is to live a life filled with rich experiences. These experiences are grounded in principles that transcend into the workplace. Wisdom is correlated to age and experiences over time; therefore, adults typically have deeper wisdom from a lifetime of experiences in all facets of life, including work and home. The behaviors related to wisdom include experience and the application of their knowledge and determination to complex, ambiguous issues. Some exemplary leaders also expressed how they are calm and assured and that although they have failed over the years, they were able to successfully learn from their mistakes and get back up. Wisdom is developed over time by rich and meaningful experiences, through setbacks as well as successes.

Again, we will discuss storytelling, supporting the fact that the 3Es remain intertwined. Exemplary leaders often use storytelling to demonstrate their wisdom and experiences. Leaders can share stories of both their successes and the challenges they have experienced. The use of stories is beneficial to help employees understand the wisdom and knowledge that a particular leader brings to the current situation. It is also through this storytelling that leaders can better understand the perspectives learned throughout their leadership journey.

Model leaders can help employees feel a sense of meaning through sharing stories of how their work is creating meaning for others. Stories of meaningfulness are powerful reminders to team members of the impact each individual employee has on the outcomes of an organization. These stories should directly align with the organization's vision, mission, and values. Meaning in the workplace will encourage employees to do what is best for all stakeholders, management, colleagues, customers, and the organization as a whole.

Not only does wisdom bring value to organizations, but it also helps leaders to understand themselves better. Wisdom also makes one aware of more complex perspectives. The Berlin Wisdom Model describes how the acquisition of wisdom comes from the efforts of establishing a "good life," achieving excellence in mind and virtue, creating meaning through life experiences, and achieving a balance between the personal and common good.[1] Through their past experiences, a leader can apply wisdom to make moral and ethical decisions. Through this wisdom, leaders can inspire followers to develop their own wisdom. Wisdom empowers an exemplary leader to lead deeply with meaning and purpose.

> "Wisdom is the reward you get for a lifetime of listening when you would rather have talked."
>
> Mark Twain

A leader's ability to share the wisdom gained through experiences via storytelling and open communication can enhance the work environment. Leaders can impact followers in the organization through the wisdom they bring to a variety of situations. It is also critical that exemplary leaders are good listeners, to add to their body of knowledge and wisdom. Again, we see the interplay with engagement. With wisdom, a leader has the potential to influence followers, the organization, and the customers that it serves. Leaders can use wisdom and past experiences as a guide to creating a meaningful workplace for themselves and their followers.

A wise leader should have clearly defined core values that guide their wisdom-building actions. An exemplary leader in our research espoused the need for careful fiduciary management. He told stories of the lean years of the organization to instill in employees an understanding of how the organization was able to build wealth. Another leader told stories of the company founding to inspire continued growth.

Simple and actionable core values are an essential element of a wise organization. Patrick Lencioni, in *The Five Dysfunctions of a Team*, stated: "Success is not a matter of mastering subtle, sophisticated theory, but rather of embracing common sense with uncommon levels of discipline and persistence."[2] Lencioni's statement indicates to us that success comes down to organizations applying a small set of practices with consistency.

Meaningful practices should be encapsulated in your core values statement, and they should be seen as essential and nonnegotiable. The core values that guide your organization should be a reflection of the leader's wisdom and be developed through collaboration. They should serve to support continued growth and success for the organization as a whole.

STRATEGIES FOR SUCCESS

Below you will find strategies for success as they relate to the development and use of wisdom. Wisdom is one key element that creates comfort and well-being for team members, especially during challenging times or periods of change. Expressing wisdom through storytelling, mentorship, and developing collaborative core values with team members are just a few strategies for success when expressing wisdom.

Storytelling

Storytelling is an effective strategy in developing a collaborative vision, but storytelling can also be effective in demonstrating wisdom by showing what has worked in the past. A leader can take several steps to ensure organizational wisdom is maximized. First, a leader must ensure they share their experience and expertise visibly for the organization to benefit. Followers expect their leaders to demonstrate wisdom. To deliver on that organizational expectation, leaders should use storytelling to share lessons learned from their experience. Additionally, they should create opportunities to demonstrate their expertise by teaching followers through sound decisions, proper conduct, and the perpetual demonstration of integrity. Put that way, you see expressing wisdom is not as simple as telling stories from the past; it is also about building the future and carefully guarding against any lapse that would be counter to the espoused core principles of the organization.

Core Values

Leaders can also build the wisdom of the organization by insisting on sound processes and procedures that guide team problem solving and decision-making. Crafted correctly, these processes and procedures serve as an extension of the leader's wisdom and invite others into the creation of organizational wisdom. This ability to deeply empower followers to solve issues creates opportunities for followers to actively pursue organizational goals guided by the core values of the organization. In this way, the core values serve as a proxy for the leader's wisdom, allowing the leader's wisdom to be omnipresent.

Mentoring

Leaders should also ensure they are mentoring followers. Mentoring allows leaders to directly share their wisdom in ways that exponentially grow organizational wisdom. By creating a process for organizational mentoring, a leader can ensure core values are kept at the forefront of conversations. Mentors are able to guide others and share actionable wisdom for others to use. Through mentoring, the leader can ensure procedures are built to develop autonomous problem solving. Mentoring can serve to deepen engagement and create an ideal environment for empowerment, while building organizational expertise.

Daily Practice

Leaders often described the need to constantly nurture and safeguard the culture of the organization. This was done in a variety of ways, several of which are listed throughout this book. The important takeaway is that the process of nurturing the culture is active and dynamic. It involves daily practice and attention to the culture and climate of the organization.

Wisdom is not a static-state goal. Organizations are shaped by many dynamic forces. Understanding and adjusting to those forces is essential for organizational health and longevity. It is essential for leaders to understand that the application of wisdom is a daily task and requires a variety of skills—safeguarding core values and insisting on sound business practices, to name just a few. Bringing your knowledge and wisdom to bear on organizational outcomes is an active practice. It requires the leader to look for signs that the organization is following a principled course and to make course corrections as necessary. The health of the organization requires leadership that is attuned to both marketplace demands and organizational actions. It is in this daily practice that a leader has the opportunity to use wisdom to guide their organization.

In summary, the ability to create an environment conducive to developing meaning can be nurtured through the sharing of wisdom. Wisdom demonstrates expertise. In the Reflection Questions for Wisdom, consider how you can relate specifically to demonstrating wisdom with colleagues. Take a few moments to consider these questions to assess your own personal growth strategies to becoming a meaning-centered leader through a display of wisdom.

Reflection Questions for Wisdom

The lessons learned from the stories I share with employees are:

The way that my actions match the elements of my stories include:

My core value statement is:

My core value statement aligns with my organization's values by:

The ways in which I demonstrate wisdom include:

Chapter 11

Optimism

At the end of the day people will forget what you said, people will forget what you did, but people will never forget how you made them feel.

—Maya Angelou

The creation of meaning is aided by an optimistic outlook on the future. Optimism is characterized by having a positive outlook and occurs when someone is hopeful about the future. An optimistic leader typically expresses oneself with positivity, trust, and confidence. In this chapter, leaders will see the importance of maintaining optimism as a key element of building meaning for themselves and their followers. More importantly, leaders who lead with optimism are creating positive health and wellness benefits for their team members. Numerous studies have verified optimism is simply good for your health!

Optimism differs from enthusiasm, which we covered in chapter 9, in some very important ways. Enthusiasm is about your daily approach to your work—the energy you are able to bring and sustain throughout the day. Enthusiasm is evident when you display the obvious signs that you truly love your work. Enthusiasm is about the here and now and the mindset of strong excitement about a situation, whereas optimism is more forward thinking.

Optimism is more about the hopefulness for the future. Optimism shows the confidence one has that there will be a successful outcome in the future. Optimism is a mindset to always see challenges as opportunities and to see the best in others—the glass-half-full versus the glass-half-empty mentality. It is also about a belief that through your work efforts, and the efforts of others around, you are truly making a positive difference in the world.

The biggest factor of optimism is plain and simple: it's good for your health! Numerous studies have shown that having a positive attitude leads to a happier, healthier you. Just google the words *optimism, optimism in the workplace,* or *optimism and health.* One simple search will glean millions upon millions of journal articles, writings, books, podcasts, and more. One recurring theme in these thousands of articles is that we, as a society, can improve our overall health and well-being by living in an optimistic space. Furthermore, since we are spending more waking hours at work, or doing work-related tasks, than we do with family or friends, it is critical to have optimism in the workplace.

One research study showed that for every ten-point increase in a person's score on their optimism scale, the risk of early death decreased by 19 percent.[1] Further studies have shown that optimism has a profound positive impact on a person's health. Optimists are better able to ward off stress, depression, anxiety, and mental and physical health issues. And if an optimist is faced with health issues, they are better able to cope with the diagnosis than a pessimist. Mindfulness practices and positivity training are becoming commonplace today and can be implemented to help employees develop an optimistic outlook.

Authors concur that the best work is performed in an environment of support, encouragement, and positivity. In fact, studies have shown that having a positive attitude filled with optimism has been proven to cause less stress, less cardiovascular disease, and greater well-being. Those living with optimism have better connections with one's environment, thereby providing the opportunity to create meaning in one's life and the lives of others around them. It is vital to the health and well-being of an organization to have leaders who have an optimistic, positive, and caring attitude.

The exemplary leaders expressed the need to have a prevailing sense of optimism. Regardless of the industry, CEOs and business leaders within the meaning research expressed the need to have an optimistic outlook on the future. Throughout the discussions regarding the ways they engaged and empowered their followers, they consistently expressed optimism. The leaders described being upbeat, positive, and cheerful. Furthermore, they expressed the need to celebrate successes and look forward with certainty that they would succeed.

The exemplary leaders described ways they build opportunities for collaborative conversations to take place to build their organizations. These conversations build connection, optimism, and meaning. Being in a community of closely connected individuals working toward common goals is a minimum expectation that the leaders expressed in interviews. They further described how these collaborative experiences bring people together and build optimism throughout the organization.

In several of the interviews, the leaders expressed the clear and compelling notion that it was their responsibility to ensure the organization is looking to the future with optimism. Some concentrated on face-to-face conversations to drive deeper optimism, while some used collective messaging. The central idea that a leader is responsible for leading others toward an optimistic future is irrefutable; however, as the leaders in our research have demonstrated, there are a variety of ways to accomplish this goal.

Not only do optimists create a better work environment, but they have the ability to look at setbacks as surmountable. Optimists look at setbacks as one single problem that is likely temporary and will be resolved with changes to the circumstances. This is very important in today's environments where change is constant and organizations must be stealth in actions to remain competitive. The ability of a leader to see a challenge as an opportunity is a sign of optimism and a positive character trait for exemplary leadership.

On the contrary, a pessimist sees setbacks as devastating and, as a result, has difficulty recovering from setbacks. Pessimists can have a negative impact on outcomes simply through the energy put forth by their attitudes. The toxicity that prevails with pessimism can be extremely detrimental to the overall health of an organization. It is very important in team settings to monitor actions, words, and behaviors of pessimists with high levels of coaching and redirecting to ensure the team as a whole can remain on task.

Optimism is critical to helping leaders rise above challenges to seek opportunities. Positive emotions and optimism can strengthen a leader's ability to solve problems and can encourage finding solutions in new and innovative ways. Martin Seligman, known as one of the leaders in positive psychology, well-being, and happiness theories, says that well-being is a construct that must be nurtured and grown. Happiness and meaning are strong factors required for the well-being of an organization.

Extraordinary, optimistic leaders will go out of their way to recognize employees in a positive fashion, whether it is on a personal or on a professional level. In fact, through his research, Martin Seligman found that companies that sustain a 2.9:1 ratio for positive to negative statements are flourishing.[2] This is a very important number to recognize and implement within your organization. Ensure that the positive comments far outweigh the negative comments at a level of three to one to thrive. Moreover, authors Bennis and Nanus shared the example of Irwin Federman, former president and chief executive officer of Monolithic Memories, who illustrated the importance of optimism wisely when he said:

> If you think about it, people love others not for who they are, but for how they make us feel. We willingly follow others for much the same reason. It makes us feel good to do so. In order to willingly accept the direction of another

individual, it must feel good to do so. This business of making another person feel good in the unspectacular course of his daily comings and goings is, in my view, the very essence of leadership.[3]

It is so true! Leaders with the heart and soul of others in mind will create a warm feeling of being a part of something bigger than oneself. Humans, in general, flourish when they feel a sense of belongingness and love.

In the book *Flourish*, Martin Seligman summarized the importance of optimism when he said, "To flourish, an individual must have all the 'core features': Positive emotions, engagement, interest, meaning, and purpose and three of the additional features: Self-esteem, optimism, resilience, vitality, self-determination, positive relationships."[4] *Meaning-Centered Leadership* can provide the tools necessary to help one flourish in their daily work.

The optimistic leader will convey messages of positivity even through uncertainty and difficult times, encouraging team members to watch for the bright side when a change is fully implemented. The positive leader will always find the silver lining and will share their enthusiasm with others. A positive attitude and a positive outlook are critical traits for a strong leader, and this optimism can inspire meaning throughout the organization.

Current trends in leadership point to the role of optimism. Optimism is clearly one of the tenets of transformational leadership. Research has found a positive correlation between a manager's use of affective commitment and inspirational leadership. Other leadership experts have described the role of optimism in creating community and helping others through difficult times.

The 1996 book by Sue Annis Hammond, *The Thin Book of Appreciative Inquiry*, presented a simple workshop approach to building positive discourse among teams. She offers that by changing from negative to positive emotion, you can actually change the way your mind thinks about a topic and build resilience. By focusing on positive emotions such as interest, curiosity, and humor, you can increase your team's performance. In her book, Hammond described a cycle of learning for organizations that focuses on positive practices and uses these experiences to move toward a positive future path. In the final analysis, Hammond describes a process where leaders use optimism to create high-performing teams.

Applying that appreciative outlook when coaching your followers is essential. Your employees need to know that their future is important to you. Whether you establish monthly mentoring sessions or just simple check-ins, employees need to see how their efforts are connected to the future of the organization. This mentorship will also allow a leader to understand the strengths, as well as the areas for development, of each team member.

Work will become easier and more rewarding if one capitalizes on the strengths of team members. By capitalizing on a strengths-based approach, with the foundation of optimism guiding these strengths, employees are able to connect to the future outlook of the organization. And as a leader, you need to understand the future outlook and convey the positive aspects with an optimistic attitude. Continued growth toward an optimistic future must be applied at the individual level if it is to be experienced at the organizational level. Now let's investigate some of the strategies for success in the development of optimism within your teams.

STRATEGIES FOR SUCCESS

Below you will find easy-to-implement strategies for expressing optimism. Optimism should not be confused with enthusiasm and recognition as it goes much deeper by demonstrating expertise and combining wisdom and knowledge. Optimism is especially effective when it is shared on a consistent schedule so that team members know what to expect. By showing optimism on a regular basis, you are reminding them of the important vision, mission, and values of your organization.

Inspirational Communication

One way to inspire team members through optimism is to start the week off right with a positive note of encouragement. One best practice is what we term the "Monday Motivators" email. Feel free to get creative on the name, be it Tuesday Tidbits, Wednesday Words of Wisdom, and so on. The important thing is to remain consistent in the time and the day that it is sent.

Monday Motivators are weekly emails whereby the leader sends a positive quote first thing of the week. By titling the email Monday Motivator, team members know exactly what to expect and they will be more likely to open it. The Monday Motivator words of encouragement are geared toward positivity, inspiration, motivation, optimism, and other tidbits of fun to start the week off on a cheerful note.

Barbara implemented Monday Motivators for years while leading teams. These Monday Motivators most often had graphics and inspirational quotes. Team members loved to read the Monday Motivators, so much so that if a week was inadvertently missed, the team members would ask what happened. This one small gesture is quick and easy to implement and is one simple way to create some happiness, well-being, and positivity throughout the organization.

Similarly, another simple-to-implement, yet extremely impactful, email is called the "Friday Follow-up." Like the Monday Motivator email, the Friday Follow-up must be focused on optimism and how the tasks throughout the past week can impact the optimistic future. Again, the subject line should read Friday Follow-up so that the team members get used to exactly what it is. The Friday Follow-up was always bulleted and contained wins and highlights from the week, some training nuggets, analysis of goals, or simple reminders—like upcoming holidays—to end the week on a positive note. The Friday Follow-up is a great way to just make sure the teams were leaving the week with some happy thoughts or new learning moments that would help all. These well-being check-ins are great ways to keep in touch with dispersed, and oftentimes siloed, groups.

Optimistic Mindset

In order to maintain an optimistic mindset, a leader needs a high degree of self-efficacy. They also need to help their followers develop a deep sense of self-efficacy. *Self-efficacy*, a term first used by psychologist Albert Bandura, simply refers to the belief one has that they have the ability to chart a course toward solving problems they encounter. In other words, if you believe you are capable of exerting influence on an outcome, then you are likely to persist in taking effective action.

Research has shown that self-efficacy increases accomplishment and well-being. Leaders can maintain high self-efficacy through ongoing goal setting and visualizing success. Visualizing success supports high performance and the lofty goals leaders set for themselves and their organizations. Having a coach, mentor, or community group that supports your goal-setting behavior is one way a leader can ensure they develop and maintain self-efficacy.

The conundrum for the leader is they are often isolated at the top. Working collectively with your leadership team to set lofty organizational goals is one way to avoid this isolation. In a recent consultation, a leader described being isolated, yet that leader was surrounded by a strong and capable leadership team. If you do not have a leadership team and collective leadership in the organization is not applicable to goal-setting situations, then a coach, mentor, or support community can help bridge that gap.

Mentors are often able to provide, through the example of their experiences, a model for accomplishment that aids the development of self-efficacy. Similarly, your followers need that example of accomplishment to develop an efficacious mindset that can lead to optimism. Leaders and followers alike need to experience success. Creating challenging goals as well as supporting the accomplishment of those goals is one way a leader can enhance the accomplishment of their teams and promote organizational optimism.

Icebreakers

A great way to create optimism is to have very short icebreakers at the start of each meeting. There are numerous short icebreaker ideas that can help start the meeting on a happy note through conversation. Further, these short icebreakers can also bring a personal touch to the group. Getting to know others on a personal level strengthens relationships and adds meaning, love, and respect for each other.

Icebreakers can be effective even if they are short and simple questions: *What's your favorite ice cream? If you could have a super power, what would it be?* Or pick a question randomly from a hat or on a piece of paper. The questions all relate to things either inside or outside of the work environment. Even on virtual meetings, these icebreakers can be implemented. Today's technology allows the asking of questions via a chat box, for example: *What brought meaning to your work this week?* For folks who are on the phone only, mics can be used and a moderator can read chats as they come in for all to hear. This takes just minutes to engage, yet can add so much optimism, positive vibes, and meaning to a meeting.

Again, to demonstrate wisdom, a leader must create a sense of optimism for the future. The interplay of the 3Es and their foundational elements can be seen throughout numerous strategies. Optimism leads employees to a vision for the future. The team has something to look forward to and to develop together. See the table titled Reflection Questions for Optimism. Take a few minutes to reflect on your experiences creating optimism, and consider areas in which you need more development.

Reflection Questions for Optimism
Examples of how I provide more positive comments throughout the day than negative (Am I nearing the 3:1 ratio?):
How do I specifically face a challenge head-on with optimism?
Specific ways that I start the week and end the week with positivity for my team members:
Examples of recent icebreakers and team builders that I have done to instill positivity among team members:

Chapter 12

Humility

> People with humility do not think less of themselves; they just think about themselves less.
>
> —Ken Blanchard, *The One Minute Manager*

The third and final element in expertise is humility. Throughout our journey describing *Meaning-Centered Leadership*, you can see the interplay of all three elements: engagement, empowerment, and expertise. Furthermore, you are likely understanding the important components within each of the 3Es. Humility is the final capstone of becoming a meaning-centered leader and, like trust, one of the more important elements.

Humility is an important leadership trait, but it is often overlooked because it is more subtle than some of the other leadership qualities. Perhaps it is a bit counterintuitive when you think about the leaders you know and the characteristics they display, but when you really consider the great leaders of all time, you will see that humility is a common leadership trait. Some of the greatest leaders of our time are known for their humility, among them are Martin Luther King, Jr., and Mother Teresa.

Numerous research studies have shown that leaders who embody humility are better listeners and are also able to inspire and motivate others more effectively. Leaders with humility appreciate the contributions others make to the team and will ensure the team is credited for their work. A humble leader has a great deal of inner confidence but remains humble in their demeanor. In fact, in the book *Good to Great*, Jim Collins said that the companies that excelled from good to great had great leaders and CEOs who demonstrated high levels of humility.

The exemplary leaders in our research identified humility as playing a role in building organizational wisdom and creating inspiration. The humble leader invites input from others and then follows up by acknowledging that input. Inviting input allows others to experience a sense of accomplishment, which deepens commitment and allows meaning to develop.

Organizational wisdom grows as the knowledge of the organization is built by others who are willing and able to share their knowledge. One of our exemplary leaders was fond of reminding his employees that they "know more about this than anyone else in the room." The implication is that they, the employees, have the knowledge and wisdom to solve the issue at hand. In turn, the employees are empowered to use the knowledge in the room to solve the issue.

The exemplary leaders described the importance of humility in a variety of ways. One leader suggested that a leader must check his or her ego at the door. Another mentioned that the leader needs to avoid focusing on their title. They described there is a difference between a leader with a big ego and a leader with a strong ego. Interestingly, one leader, a self-described alpha, described the constant struggle to be humble with the need to also be practical.

Throughout the interviews, exemplary leaders demonstrated the need to express their humility. By recognizing the contributions of others in meetings and communications, they are humbly expressing that the organizational success being celebrated is about the team members. By acknowledging they are not the ones with all the answers and seeking feedback, they are empowering others through their humble approach. Several of the leaders described how they expressed to their teams the need for constant improvement. This act alone expresses a humble opinion, that while we may be doing well, we can always do better.

Simon Sinek described the importance of humility as the ability for the leader to distribute power throughout the organization. This level of humility strengthens the organizational survivability by preventing dependence on a singular leader. Kouzes and Posner referred to this as "the legacy of many."[1]

In their 2017 publication *Humility Is the New Smart*, Hess and Ludwig describe four fundamental behaviors necessary for humility: quieting ego, managing self, reflective listening, and otherness (emotionally connecting and relating to others). The authors contend, "To be New Smart is to excel at the highest level of thinking, learning, and emotionally engaging with others that one is capable of doing." They go on to add, "To mitigate ego and fear and excel at the highest levels of human thinking and emotional engagement requires a new mindset that embraces humility."[2]

Additional recent research has uncovered that humility and empowerment have a high impact on worker satisfaction. When focusing on humility among CEOs, research shows that leaders who express the purpose and the vision are able to effectively show humility, even while receiving feedback, and even criticism, from others. A humble leader knows that others can help them to build the overall vision more effectively. Executive search teams and executive coaching should consider humility as a trait worthy of consideration.

Moreover, research has linked leadership humility to developing shared leadership among teams. When leaders demonstrate a willingness to learn from others and publicly praise their followers, they help to build team member reliance. This, in turn, builds the capacity for team members to take the lead when their teams need their expertise.

Humble leaders demonstrate through their actions that they have a growth mindset. By being willing and able to learn from others, they demonstrate the important trait of lifelong learning that is associated with a growth mindset. Experts in the field who fail to maintain a growth mindset will not be experts for very long. When leaders listen to followers and show that they are open to new ideas, they demonstrate their willingness to learn from others. An organization that is constantly learning will increase its competitive advantage in the long run.

Humility is not often discussed in daily conversation as a leadership trait to seek because people may consider this word to describe someone as passive, meek, or weak, but in reality, this is not the case. The term *humility* is a bit nebulous; the opposite of humility is not! Think of it this way: How do you feel about a leader who is narcissistic, self-centered, arrogant, conceited, egotistical? Would you want to work for or with someone with these traits? Likely not. In fact, you would likely run away from a job if someone said, "This narcissist will be your boss!"

Again, the opposite of the adjectives like *narcissism* and *arrogance* is *humility*. Leaders who display humility are not self-centered. Humble leaders are servant leaders. Humble leaders look out for others and for the success of the organization as a whole. Humble leaders are trustworthy and authentic. They do not act as if they are the smartest in the room but instead support their followers to share in the responsibility for the successes. A humble leader knows that teamwork makes the dream work! A humble leader includes others in successes yet takes responsibility for failures. In our research, one exemplary university president stated, "You must be humble and, in fact, humility and wisdom go hand-in-hand."

In an article from the *Harvard Business Review*, Dame and Gedmin suggest that developing leaders need to focus on six important behaviors. First, "Know What You Don't Know." Rely-on-others versus a master-of-the-universe approach. Next, "Resist Falling for Your Own Publicity"; it can cloud your judgment. Third, "Never Underestimate the Competition." The world is full of intelligent, innovative, hardworking people. Fourth, "Embrace and Promote a Spirit of Service." Your employees need to know you care about their success. Fifth, "Listen, Even, (No, Especially) to the Weird Ideas." You never know what great ideas are waiting to be shared. Finally, "Be Passionately Curious." Take it from Einstein. "I have no special talent," he claimed. "I am only passionately curious."[3]

In the foreward to the 25th Anniversary edition of Robert Greenleaf's book *Servant Leadership*, Stephen Covey explained that, in his experience, the top people in great organizations are the humblest people. He stated, "When people with the formal authority or positional power refuse to use that authority and power, except as a last resort, their moral authority increases because it is obvious that they have subordinated their ego and positional power and use reasoning, persuasion, kindness, empathy, and in short, trustworthiness instead."[4] Covey goes on to explain his belief that enlightened leadership has the power to heal our country. That leadership must be grounded by a leader who has the humility to be more concerned with building others than commanding them.

"Our age of arrogance obscures the idea that humility is the indispensable virtue for the achievement of greatness. . . . to be truly great, one has to be humble."[5] The enlightened leadership called for by Stephen Covey in the preceding paragraph is illustrated in this statement from David Bobb, author of *Humility: An Unlikely Biography of America's Greatest Virtue*. Against the backdrop of several great American historical figures, Bobb points out that humility allows for courage to take place. Further, Bobb states that humility sets wisdom in the right direction. He also notes that humility is hard to achieve. Humility requires deep self-knowledge, especially for those who assume themselves to be great. Perhaps the best piece of advice to be extracted from Bobb's work is the idea he offers that humility is a practice: "Humility is a quality of the soul that cannot be perfected but can be practiced."[6] With that in mind, we offer the following strategies for success that will aid you in the practice of humility.

STRATEGIES FOR SUCCESS

Humility is an important trait to develop, but it is oftentimes difficult to define and to practice. Humility tends to develop over time, through knowledge-building and hard work, with a specific focus on self-reflection. Below we outline some specific strategies for displaying your own level of humility, including working hard to always credit others before self for a job well done, admitting your own mistakes, consistently working on self-development, and inviting input from others. Humble leaders are great leaders! Be sure to honestly assess your own level of humility when you work on the resources for change in the following chapters.

Credit Others

A leader who displays humility will reward and recognize team members before self. This is an important leadership trait and will inspire team members to follow such a leader to great heights. Followers love to be rewarded and recognized for their work, and a humble leader will be sure to include them loud and clear when praising success for a project or task. This positivity breeds greater positivity, and the team thrives.

Consider the example of Steve Kerr, coach of the three-time NBA champions, the Golden State Warriors. From his days as a professional basketball player with both the Chicago Bulls and the San Antonio Spurs to his more recent coaching years, Kerr continues to act and lead with humility.

Throughout his career, Steve Kerr has been praised for his coaching and his winning attitude. He has a strong ethical belief in doing what's right, no matter what. Further, when repeatedly praised for his coaching skills, Kerr states that it is a team effort. He consistently emphasizes the importance of building his team of leaders so the team can work in partnership with each other, even in the absence of one.

For years, Kerr's humility has shone through in the players he has developed and the humility they each display. Kerr has also held his coaches to the same standard, coaching with humility and empowering others. Most importantly, Kerr displays his humility in the interviews conducted after each game! Not only does Kerr state that it was a team effort, he publicly thanks and appreciates players and leaders alike for taking him to the level of success he has achieved. Basically, his successes are not self-focused; they are other-focused and come from a space of gratitude, appreciation, and humility.

Conversely, consider the opposite of a humble leader. Likely each and every person reading this book can relate to leaders who are everything but humble! This is the type of leader most of us dread: the leader who toots their own horn first and foremost, the leader who publicly announces their own successes to their uplines, forgetting to even mention the hard work from their team members below them, the leader who immediately blames others if a goal is not met, pointing fingers at their own downlines and other departments within the organization. This type of toxic leader is typically incapable of ever crediting others.

Admit Mistakes

Humility gives a leader the strength and fortitude to admit their own mistakes. In fact, oftentimes a truly humble leader will take responsibility for the full situation, even if the blame falls on others, because, in fact, it is the leader who is the ultimate one in charge and he or she knows it. When a leader admits mistakes, they demonstrate vulnerability. As we discussed in chapter 4, by showing vulnerability, leaders can build that capacity among their followers. This allows the leader to create an environment where humility is seen as an organizational virtue.

Develop Self

A humble leader knows that constant improvement and learning is required of all, including themself. They know their strengths and they understand their weaknesses. A humble leader is willing to ask for feedback and will take measures to make improvements in growth. A humble leader is not afraid of a 360° Assessment because they are confident enough to know that positive and constructive feedback will only allow their qualities and skills to improve. By admitting that they do not know everything, a humble leader instills creativity, openness, and confidence in their team members.

In addition to 360° Assessments and other self-development tools, a humble leader will oftentimes find a confidant within the organization. This coach, and trusted advisor, is someone whom they can ask for honest and authentic feedback. This person is someone who knows for sure that, no matter what they say, there will not be repercussions from the feedback provided. This relationship is so strongly bonded that the confidant can share the good, the bad, and the ugly. This is critical to self-development, especially for the top leaders in an organization. The confidant must be able to approach the leader at any point in time and provide feedback that will allow a true and honest assessment of a situation. By having this trusted relationship, even the top leader in an organization can stay on track, grow their strengths, and improve upon their weaknesses.

Invite Input

A humble leader is ready and willing to have ideas and input from all team members. It is from this information exchange and open-door policy that a leader can demonstrate that they may not be the only one with insight. One way a leader can invite input is by creating that deep environment of trust, as discussed previously. Without trust, input will not be provided. Further, through coaching and conversations, the leader can use every opportunity to hear about, and from, others. If the humble leader follows through with regular MBWA techniques and listens intently and authentically to followers, it opens the door to also allow the leader to ask for feedback.

One example can be seen in the scenario where a leader is walking around. As they casually stop to chat with a colleague, they can end the conversation like this: *Hey, thank you for speaking with me today. May I ask you a question? Can you provide me with honest feedback?* Likely the team member will agree. This is where the leader can then ask for feedback or input: *Is there anything that I can do differently to make your job easier? Is there something you feel I can improve upon to be a better leader for your team? Is there something I could have handled differently?* They can even ask about a particular meeting or scenario.

As a leader asks this question time and time again, the team members will become used to the question, and it will get easier over time for the team members to respond more honestly. Now, one important element of asking for this type of feedback is taking the feedback with grace and with no retribution, no matter what is stated. Receive feedback with the upmost of humility. Use these opportunities to grow and reflect. Do not use these opportunities to trap colleagues. Meaning is created with this level of honesty and humility. As you consider your Reflection Questions for Humility, ask yourself how you can become a meaning-centered, humble leader.

Reflection Questions for Humility

How do I recognize and reward team members with humility when a project is complete?

When a project falls apart, how do I hold myself accountable?

Specific ways I demonstrate vulnerability include:

I recognize others in the workplace by:

SUMMARY OF EXPERTISE

The words from the 2016 song "Humble and Kind," written by Lori McKenna and sung by artist Tim McGraw, sums up the chapter on expertise, and *Meaning-Centered Leadership*, quite well when they mention that a person should just be a good human being by behaving with respect, appreciation, and humility. The words in the song sum up what it means to take a meaning-focused approach to your behaviors and your leadership style. One must be humble and kind to increase engagement, empowerment, and expertise.

Expertise through wisdom, optimism, and humility begins through the interplay of engagement and empowerment. Just build strong relationships; let your employees know they are respected, appreciated, and loved. Encourage them through recognition and enthusiasm, and show your expertise to be their guiding light. It all boils down to just being a good human and an exemplary leader, a leader who creates organizational meaning for themselves and their organization.

Part IV

MEASURING MEANING

BECOMING A MEANING-CENTERED LEADER

What gets measured gets managed.

—Peter Drucker, *The Practice
of Management*

In his 1954 book *The Practice of Management*, Peter Drucker so eloquently wrote the above quote. Nearly seventy years later, this statement continues to be repeated. We believe these words hold true to measuring and managing the impact of your leadership. In this part of the book, we offer tools for measuring your impact and deepening your practice as a meaning-centered leader. You may already measure the impact of your leadership in terms of sales, test scores, new clients, and so on, but by taking the time to measure the impact of your *Meaning-Centered Leadership* behaviors, you build your skills toward improving the potential to take your outcomes to new heights.

As we have established, meaning has the capacity to drive your followers to deeper commitment, better performance, and improved well-being. By taking the next step to measure your impact, examine data, reflect on your practices, and set goals for improvement, you can increase your *Meaning-Centered Leadership* score (MCL score).

In chapter 13 we offer resources for change: straightforward practices informed by research that will help you increase engagement, strengthen empowerment, and deepen your expertise. By focusing on simple, yet tried-and-true, leadership behaviors that strengthen your potential for creating meaning, you create the opportunity to build meaning for yourself, your followers, and your organization.

A meaning-centered organization experiences trusting relationships that are expressed in collaborative work toward a compelling future. If that is the type of organization you wish to lead, you should take the time to build your skills. Engagement, empowerment, and expertise are constructs that can be measured and improved upon on a daily basis.

Daily check-ins and self-reflective practices will ensure your *Meaning-Centered Leadership* techniques do not become just another New Year's resolution, falling by the wayside by January 31. As we already know, "What gets measured gets managed." In chapter 14 we present the *Meaning-Centered Leadership* Personal Inventory Assessment. This tool will measure your MCL score so you can manage your leadership behaviors to maximize meaning in your organization. We also introduce our *Meaning-Centered Leadership* 360° Assessment (MCL-360°). The MCL-360° Assessment is available on our website. This tool is for those leaders who wish to take a deeper look at their leadership impact. The MCL-360° Assessment provides feedback from multiple sources to provide a closer inspection of your leadership development.

Meaning-Centered Leadership concludes with chapter 15, offering a call to action and reminder that the journey to becoming a meaning-centered leader is a lifelong pursuit.

Chapter 13

Resources for Change

Without continual learning, we'll soon fall behind.

—Scott Mautz, *Make It Matter*

The modern world requires us to embrace lifelong learning and a growth mindset. For leaders, this viewpoint is essential. Leaders need to add value to their own development as well as to their followers' development. In fact, the Gallup research has found that today's workforce requires professional development as an opportunity when joining an organization. Today's workforce wants to stay relevant and knowledgeable, and it is a leader's job, and an organization's obligation, to provide such development.

One sure way to continue to learn and grow is to constantly feed your mind with new and relevant information. With that in mind, we will offer several resources for change in this chapter. You will find information that will help you build meaning with your team and organization, including developing your personal vision statement and structuring devices, sample meeting agendas, reflective journal prompts, and additional resources for becoming a meaning-centered leader.

First, we will begin by developing your personal vision statement. Your vision statement can address the impact or legacy you want to leave. We will then cover meeting structures to help you build your potential to engage and empower followers while maximizing the opportunities to use your expertise to influence positive outcomes for your organization. Next, we offer an array of self-reflective journal prompts to grow your self-reflective practices. You have seen some of these journal prompts throughout the text, but here you will find a cumulative document for ease of reference. Finally, we present an array of books, articles, and podcasts to deepen your knowledge on the impact of meaning on your leadership. The body of research and insight we have gained from our fellow authors and colleagues has been invaluable in the development of our theory. We hope that you enjoy some of these additional resources as you improve upon your knowledge, skills, and abilities to create meaning in your organization.

DEVELOPING YOUR MEANINGFUL VISION STATEMENT

Before you can implement change, you have to know where you are going. A good start to finding out where you are going is to write your own personal and meaningful vision statement. You will see some guiding journal prompts. It is important to start with the larger picture of your dreams, goals, and aspirations. Consider things you love and what fulfills you. Consider your passions and your fears. What makes you happy? Finally, your vision statement can be developed. It should be succinct and actionable.

Make your answers brief and succinct, and then look for connections to others. Bind those connections with the actions you need to take to bring your vision to fruition. When building your personal vision statement, look for ideas from others. For example, Oprah Winfrey's vision statement: "To be a teacher. And to be known for inspiring my students to be more than they thought they could be."[1] Notice the others in Oprah's statement: her students. Her statement makes it clear that she is serving someone. It also describes how she serves: by teaching.

Developing Your Personal Vision Statement

My goals, dreams, and aspirations today are:

Specific details of how my goals and aspirations have changed over the years include:

The things I can do today to make the impact I want to leave behind as a legacy for others include:

I find my meaning and purpose through:

Things that motivate me include:

My succinct personal vision statement looks like this:

Your statement might also express how you intend to accomplish a lofty goal. For example, the vision statement of CEO of Campbell's Soup Denise Morgan is "To serve as a leader, live a balanced life, and apply ethical principles to make a significant difference."[2] Her statement describes her intention to be a leader who maintains balance while following an ethical path. On the contrary, your statement might describe your intention to seek certain outcomes. Richard Branson's vision statement—"To have fun in my journey through life and learn from my mistakes"[3]—makes clear his intention to have fun.

Whether you choose to serve others, serve your god, or simply want to have fun and learn like Richard Branson, your vision statement should be a short one-to-two-sentence description of your intentions. As you can see from the three vastly different statements shared here, your statement is as individual as you are. Your vision statement should connect your values and skills to an action that you prefer.

According to Viktor Frankl, two ways we can discover meaning in life is through creating a work or doing a deed and by experiencing something or encountering someone. Look for these elements in your vision statement. Examine your statement for work and experiences that you enjoy. How does your statement plot a course for you to interact with the world in a way that allows for you to accomplish what is most important to you? Does your vision statement specify the work you will do and those you will impact?

Your personal vision statement must rest on a foundational belief that you deserve a life full of meaningful work—work that connects to your strengths and core values. It is important to remember that your personal vision statement may seem out of reach or express some future state. It is exactly that yearning for a future state, a future state worthy of your efforts, that will bring meaning to your work and your life. However, this yearning for a future state will not happen without the hard work of consistent goal setting, goals that lead you to your future state.

One way to gain focus on this future state is to visualize your future five years from today. Not only visualize but write down your visualizations in a clear five years in the future journal reflection. This five-year forward projection should excite you with the potential it presents. It should represent what can be accomplished if you are focused on continual personal development and living by a code of ethics.

Your personal vision statement should guide you toward your five-year projection. The difference between your current state and the future state should provide ample opportunities for you to identify goals that need to be met to accomplish this future state. This is where the heavy lifting starts, where you go from envisioning to creating. Goal setting and constant reflection on the progress you are making are necessary. Without these steps, your future state will simply be a daydream. Acknowledging the hard work that exists between your current and future states is imperative. This distance will only be closed by consistently setting goals and accurately monitoring the completion of those goals. The hard work to close this distance will not only allow you to find great meaning in your work and life; it will aid your ability to be a meaning-centered leader.

MEETING STRUCTURES

Leaders often struggle with creating meetings that inspire and engage their teams. Why else would meetings be the butt of so many jokes and cartoons? In his book *Meetings Matter: 8 Powerful Strategies for Remarkable Conversations*, Paul Axtell mentions, "While nearly everyone who is asked will tell you they hate meetings, I don't think that's the case at all. I think people simply get frustrated wasting valuable time they could spend more productively elsewhere." It is your job as the leader to ensure that meeting time strengthens relationships, leads to enhanced productivity, and allows you to deepen the opportunity for meaning to grow in your organization.

Meetings for the sake of having a meeting, or meetings with little or no follow-up, do not provide a clear purpose or path. Meetings have the power to engage, empower, and build expertise, but without careful planning and thoughtful facilitation, meetings can drain energy and create dissent and disengagement.

A leader must put time and energy into each and every one of their meetings. Careful planning with the end result in mind is essential. Further, it is critical to follow through and follow up on meeting agendas and the related outcomes. The measurability of the meeting outcomes will determine the success of future meetings. An organization simply cannot continue to have meetings just for the sake of having meetings.

If you have ever sat through meetings that require you to listen to information that would have been better delivered via email, you know what we mean. However, if you use the 3Es model for structuring your meetings, you are sure to create productive meetings that build team engagement, empower followers, and build organizational expertise. For example, imagine your meetings starting with the goal of engaging teams in fun and energizing collaborative activities or opportunities to share professional or personal successes. The larger the meeting, the more challenging this can be, but even large groups can participate in success and idea share in smaller groups, and then report back to the team as a whole.

The result of structuring this interaction at the start of the meeting makes your meeting rooms friendlier places that exponentially grow positive emotions and deepen connections between teams. These moments create the opportunity for meaning via engagement to deepen and grow. In small meetings of six to twelve people, you can simply start by using a *whip around* to share a personal or professional "Good Things." A whip around is where you give a short prompt and quickly give each person at the table an opportunity to share a good thing that has happened to them. Good things always put a smile on the participants' faces and it allows an opportunity for relationships to strengthen. Team members can get to know each other better through the shared answers. As the leader and facilitator, you signal to your followers that they are more important than the brass tacks that populate the agenda.

These short icebreakers, or whip-around prompts, can change at each meeting. Below are a few great whip-around prompts:

1. Good Thing: Share a personal or professional good thing that happened to you this week.
2. Meaning: Share your most meaningful moment at work this week.
3. Feel good: What has happened at work this week that made you feel really great about what you do day-in and day-out?
4. What's your "job"?: Describe in five words what is your job? (Note: Participants are to explain what they do, not their title).
5. Favorites: What is your favorite (color, dessert, summer activity, animal, free time activity, movie, book . . .)?

In larger groups of fifteen to thirty, it is easy to do similar activities simply by breaking up into smaller groups and then offer each group the opportunity to share one thing they discussed. The result is similar and engagement at the table ensues. Large groups doing energizer activities can help to lessen the apprehension the participants may be feeling while creating a positive buzz. Large group activities can be done creatively to target a specific issue or just to build a positive esprit de corps. In large groups, you are not only building positive emotions but also creating opportunities for individuals who may not work together all the time to interact and build relationships with each other.

A case in point, several years ago, Ed worked for a transformational leadership team in a high-performing school district in Dublin, California. The superintendent and associate superintendent co-facilitated a monthly leadership team meeting comprised of every certificated and classified leader in the district. Everyone, from site principals to the head of maintenance, attended. In terms of the jobs, it was quite a diverse group. Each meeting began with an energizer/icebreaker.

As a new leader in the district, Ed, through these meetings, was able to meet everyone on the district leadership team. The meetings helped him build relationships, which in turn deepened engagement within the organization. During these meetings, the facilitators took time for recognition and built buy-in on initiatives via collaborative visioning. The enthusiasm for the work was always at a fever pitch in these meetings. As a result, the leadership team exited the meetings empowered and energized.

Each meeting typically had an educational component. Perhaps most importantly, the facilitators expressed deep appreciation for the team's work. They always reminded us that without our efforts the district would not be a high-performing institution that took exceptional care of the students of Dublin. With humility on full display, the superintendent greeted us when we entered, and said good-bye as we left, always thanking us for our work. The meetings never veered from an optimistic course. The wisdom of the organization deepened with each meeting. Employees felt valued and were reminded that each job had a specific meaning and purpose.

Unlike the scenario in Dublin, many employees at other organizations have expressed their disdain for meetings, including leaders! And this certainly should come as no surprise. It is likely that you have also experienced such frustrations.

Team members have different reasons for feeling negative about meetings. Perhaps it is due to years of being an audience participant in meetings that did little to engage and/or empower them. Maybe it is due to the work of structuring the meeting or a discomfort with being on stage. Perhaps team members are tired of listening to the same old "talking heads," as some employees have described. One person interviewed stated that meetings tend to be monologues with speakers that appear to be the select few from the favorite of the month club members, repeating their same best practices over and over again. The point is, every time you gather in a meeting, you have the opportunity to deepen engagement, empower your teams, and use your expertise to build wisdom and to create meaning in your organization. Do not let this slip away through meetings that add no value to the lives of your team members.

For meetings to be effective and worthwhile, there must not just be the same few people at the head of the table in a didactic monologue, directing what they believe to be best practices or opportunities for success. Instead, effective meetings must be engaging and collaborative, with open conversation and input from all members. All meeting participants should feel safe and comfortable stating their thoughts, positions, opinions, concerns, and accolades. There should be no fear of providing open and honest dialogue, even if it is hard to hear at times. Leaders need to embrace meetings as an opportunity to deepen organizational meaning for themselves and their followers.

By using the *Meaning-Centered Leadership* framework to guide the construction of your agenda, you can build meetings that engage, empower, and deepen the wisdom in your organization. Let's break that down step by step. Each meeting should be composed of the following stages, with equal attention to each:

1. An affirmative greeting
2. An icebreaker or energizer
3. A focus on the organizational vision: the Unifier
4. Clearly stated goals and outcomes for the meeting
5. A value-added or educational component
6. An opportunity for dialogue to build clarity
7. Clearly defined next steps and expectations
8. A positive send-off

Taking the time to honor the attendance of your employees by greeting them with an affirmation of their presence personalizes the meeting experience. You have likely experienced a leader who stands at the podium and waits for everyone to enter, and then launches into his/her agenda. Those meetings are largely a waste of time. The employees in the audience are often completing other tasks on their cell phones and may even be openly disengaged. Employee morale and behavior suffer as a result.

Witnessing these types of behaviors as a member of the organization where such behavior took place, it was clear that the lack of leadership invited much of the chaos that ensued. The organization opens itself up to lawsuits related to unscrupulous employee behavior. With each meeting, the leader behind the podium affirmed that we were an organization without standards, little to no discipline, and zero respect for the leadership.

Leaders who fail to attend to meeting structures and employee behavior within those meetings are inviting disengagement at a ruinous level. On the contrary, the leader who carefully attends to creating meetings that build relationships, and deepen connection and engagement within the organization, can build the collective wisdom of the organization, and can position appropriate outcomes.

It is imperative that you carefully develop meeting agendas that build your organization and its employees up. A carefully constructed agenda can keep your meeting on-track and avoid derailments that can sometimes occur. We all have likely experienced a meeting where an individual agenda gets brought to the collective group and there is a disruptor. However, as the meeting facilitator, you will need to cautiously guard against these meeting disruptions. Redirecting off-topic diatribes is an essential skill.

Oftentimes a leader must let people know that the topic they brought up is not on the agenda, and it will be discussed at a later date. By stating an objective upfront, and using your agenda to drive conversation, you will have given yourself tools for interrupting the interrupter. The meeting facilitator must be able to move the conversation along the agenda and in the direction of the stated goals of the meeting. Simply being able to refocus with a phrase that directs everyone back to the goals and the agenda is often enough to restore the potential for collective good. It may also be necessary to coach team members outside of the meeting on appropriate meeting decorum. In order for the meeting to be the important touch point it can be, the leader must carefully ensure that the collective interest of the participants is being served.

Establishing the expected decorum in meetings is essential. It allows you to declare the rules of the game. The behind-the-podium meeting leader never established the rules for the meetings they facilitated. As a result, it was anything goes. Establishing rules and reviewing them at the start of the meeting is essential. For example, all meeting agendas should begin with the norms and protocols, as well as a list of the professional and ethical dispositions (see example). Moreover, these protocols should be quickly reviewed at the beginning of each meeting. Your essential elements may vary, but you must declare the rules of engagement.

Meeting Norms & Protocols	Professional & Ethical Dispositions
Start on time and end on time Stick to the agenda No side-bar conversations Cell phones on silent Solution-focused Agreement by consensus	As an educator we value the worth and dignity of every person, the pursuit of truth, devotion to excellence, acquisition of knowledge, and the nurture of democratic citizenship.

Next, your norms and protocols, as well as the agenda items, should be reviewed and affirmed by the group at the start of the meeting. A carefully designed agenda, with input from essential team members, will allow you to gain quick consensus at the outset. Once that consensus is gained, it is much more difficult for a meeting to be derailed. As you design your agendas, be mindful to ensure the meeting agenda essentials have been carefully considered.

REFLECTIVE JOURNAL PROMPTS

A humble leader knows there is always room for growth and improvement. An authentic and meaning-centered leader takes the time to assess a variety of situations and reflect upon these moments to see if there are ways to improve their own personal leadership. In fact, having a confidant or a coach is a great way to monitor your own personal development opportunities. Throughout the book, we provided journal prompts on which to reflect. Below is a comprehensive list of reflection questions to inspire your own personal growth and development.

1. How do I engage my employees on a regular basis?
2. What do I do to specifically build trusting relationships?
3. How do I connect on a personal level with employees?

4. Do I know the "basics" about my employees (or at least my first- and second-level direct reports)? This includes family, hobbies, pets, vacations, likes/dislikes, and so on.
5. How do I show others that I care about their well-being? Is it clear and compelling?
6. Does my caring light the way to a brighter future?
7. Does my care and concern align with our core values?
8. Was my organization's vision developed collaboratively?
9. Do I uphold the vision through actions, words, and decision-making throughout the organization?
10. Is our workplace setup conducive to open, honest, and authentic conversations?
11. Have I had any meaningful conversations with my team members lately? Do I know what is frustrating them, what keeps them up at night, what are their dreams, and where do they want to go in the organization?
12. Is my office in the ivory tower, or can I get real and be on the ground floor with the troops?
13. When was the last time I answered the phones at the front desk or taken on another task on "the front line" within my organization?
14. When was the last time I spoke directly to an end-user of our product?
15. When was the last time I practiced management by walking around?
16. Do I have monthly or, at a maximum, quarterly meetings with my direct reports to simply discuss goals, dreams, and aspirations?
17. Do I provide more positive comments throughout the day than negative?
18. How close am I to the 3:1 ratio recommended in the literature for positive comments?
19. When confronted with a challenge, do I face it head-on with an attitude of optimism that we will succeed in obtaining positive outcomes?
20. Have I built in enough icebreakers or team builders to instill positivity in our culture?
21. Do I begin and end the week with positivity for my team members?

CORE VALUES STATEMENT

The recent declaration by the 181 CEOs of the Business Roundtable who signed onto *The Statement on the Purpose of a Corporation* acknowledged that workers deserve meaning and dignity in the workplace. Valuing the input of all stakeholders must be considered when developing core values. It requires that your personal and organizational core values are aligned to this new reality. As mentioned in chapter 10, core values express wisdom and should guide an organization's development of processes and procedures. Leaders must focus their efforts on results. Those processes and procedures must focus on bringing meaning to the workplace. Meaning-centered leaders must ensure those results include building organizational meaning.

Examine your organizational values for alignment with the elements of leadership we have described in this book. Those elements will allow you and your organization to determine if you have a focus on outcomes associated with the creation of meaning. The aforementioned declaration by the Business Roundtable made the following statement: "Investing in our employees. This starts with compensating them fairly and providing important benefits. It also includes supporting them through training and education that help develop new skills for a rapidly changing world. We foster diversity and inclusion, dignity and respect."[4]

This statement within the declaration creates action items for leaders to follow. The path to meaning can be seen in this statement. Training, education, and skill development are all facets of the *Meaning-Centered Leadership* theory. Coaching, mentoring, dignity, and respect are foundations of engagement, empowerment, and expertise, as outlined in this book.

More importantly, it is critical that all stakeholders within your organization not only know the organization's core values but practice the core values. When an organization has employees who do not align with the core values, the decline of culture, and therefore engagement and productivity, occurs rapidly.

The leader's task is to create a core values statement that is collaborative, is practiced, and aligns with the very important business-related outcomes. Further, the leader must focus on the results of these outcomes with equal resilience and resolve. Accepting outcomes that fall short of promoting meaning will short-circuit the leader's efforts to create a meaning-centered organization.

The research indicates that leaders who fail to place meaning and purpose at the core of organizational strategies fail to maximize the organization's potential. By placing a focus on creating a meaning-centered organization, you put a focus on the very important soft skills of leadership that are often overlooked.

Soft skills were frequently cited in the research on why people leave their jobs. These skills include relationships, trust, care and concern, and other elements presented in this book. When people fail to experience trust and autonomy, they fail to experience engagement and empowerment. This failure is one major reason employees take the next step of disengagement and they leave their jobs. The leader must ensure that the core values of the organization are a central fabric of the operations within the organization. The meaning-centered approach must be operationalized in terms of specific actions.

To build a meaning-centered approach, a leader can begin by following the strategies outlined in this book. They must also make meaning a central part of their meeting agendas and leadership training. By owning this approach through direct actions taken by leadership, others in the organization will realize that the behaviors associated with creating meaning are valuable and an essential element of the organization. As you have witnessed by examples of the contrary throughout this book, by not following a *Meaning-Centered Leadership* approach, the organization's overall success could be at risk.

Leaders who take time to ensure their leadership teams understand *Meaning-Centered Leadership* will see more immediate results. As the *Meaning-Centered Leadership* approach is used throughout the organization, it will move from static words on a value statement to desired actions and results throughout the organization. All stakeholders, including those millennial and Gen Z employees who seek deep meaning in their work, will be inspired to renew their commitments.

A quick examination of award-winning American companies allows you to see the connection between core values, mission, vision, and the strong culture that has been created. Before you take the important steps to build a culture that focuses on a meaning-centered approach, you must align your core values to the outcomes you desire. Take, for example, the core values of JetBlue, one of America's most competitive airlines and a 2017 Best Places to Work award winner: *safety, caring, integrity, passion,* and *fun.* As you can see, their core values are active descriptors. They describe how work will be accomplished, with fun, passion, and safety in mind. The values further align by how they will treat each other with care. Finally, integrity describes an overarching emphasis on truth and transparency.

A leader's core values must be found in their core value statement. That statement must further align with the mission and vision in actionable ways. Values that describe the work that is to be accomplished is essential to managing strategy decisions, leading change, and promoting an environment that values all stakeholders.

We suggest taking the following steps in developing a core values statement that includes a *Meaning-Centered Leadership* focus.

Core Value Development	Notes
List	The values that are essential for me and my organization include:
Collaborate	Values my colleagues and stakeholders find important include:
Share	Share with board members and community members for input.
Discuss	Discuss how the core values match the company goals with a meaning-centered approach.
Clarify	How do the values support operational practices?

Once your core values have been crafted and linked to your vision and mission, the important work of communicating those values begins. They must be present in operational documents, in your conversations with others, and in your daily actions. Think back to the JetBlue values; focusing on a simple set of operational values takes clarity and consistency. Your core values list means nothing but wasted time unless you enact them operationally.

YOUR COACHING PLAYBOOK

Throughout this book we have talked about the importance of coaching your teams. Great organizations typically have great leadership training. Coaching is an essential skill that leaders must develop to help their organizations grow. Some organizations choose outside coaches, and that is a direction you can take to develop your organization. However, the basics of coaching others should be in your leadership repertoire.

Foundational to your coaching should be the understanding that as a coach, you help others find the answers. The trainee must be considered as the expert with the answers. The coach's central role is to help the trainee find truth and objectivity when they examine their own behavior. One way a coach does this is through helping the trainee see opportunities they may not see on their own. It is essential that you understand that your role as a coach is to help others identify ways that they can solve things for themselves. Coaching is not about being the answer expert; it is about clarifying the issues and helping others find their priorities. This is not a process with a clear road map. The process can be ambiguous, and the coach must be able to handle the uncertainty.

Your goal as a coach is to develop the tools that the trainee already has. Effective coaching challenges the trainee to question their own thinking and discover new ways to solve problems. The relationship that is built within the context of coaching can become a catalyst for change. Change can occur for the trainee, the coach, and the organization.

As a coach you must become adept at asking open-ended questions that provide greater insight. A typical coaching conversation needs to peel back layers of the onion to dig deeper into the thoughts that underlie actions. For example, "Can you explain why that outcome is important?" A simple statement such as "Tell me more" may generate the deeper insight you are looking for as a coach. Without understanding these underlying thoughts, your coaching sessions will simply be corrective conversations about observed experiences. Your goal as a coach is to help others see the connection between their actions and the outcomes those actions provoke.

In summary, your approach to coaching should:

- Include an approach that assumes the trainee has the answers they need.
- Include a focus on a decision-making process that is effective from an organizational and personal viewpoint.
- Contain a rationale for decisions that is explicit and supported by data/research.
- Be a collaborative partner in planning.
- Provide formative feedback.
- Demonstrate the connection between theory and practice.

REFERENCE MATERIALS

In the next chapter we present tools for measuring your impact as a meaning-centered leader. After you have completed the personal inventory and devoted time to the reflection journals, you will be ready to set leadership goals designed to increase your ability to bring meaning to your organization.

Wherever you are on your leadership journey, constant growth and personal development are essential. We have selected several resources to help you on that journey. Along with the reflective practices, personal inventories, and authors mentioned in the book, we have provided a list of resources for you to target your growth and deepen your impact.

The list is drawn from our research and constant growth as leaders and researchers. You will find the list is laid out like our book, beginning with resources to deepen your understanding of the impact of meaning and moving on to specific elements of leadership within the 3Es framework. Other great resources can be found in the bibliography.

Books that describe the quest for meaning and why it matters

- *Man's Search for Meaning*, 1946, by Viktor E. Frankl. We highly recommend this book as it is one of the more timeless classics on meaning. This is a short book with a long impact. The author describes three paths to finding meaning in life. This is an essential read to understand how meaning supports our survival. The book also brought the age-old quest of the search for meaning into the twentieth century. In times of struggle and change, it is more important than ever to remember the reasons for living life to its fullest.
- *The Power of Meaning: Finding Fulfillment in a World Obsessed with Happiness*, 2017, by Emily Esfahani Smith. This book provides an illuminating vision of how meaning needs to be discovered in our lives if we hope to find fulfilling experiences. The author uses stories from the past and the present to guide the reader's understanding of the long human quest to find meaning.

- *Authentic Happiness: Using the New Positive Psychology to Realize Your Potential for Lasting Fulfillment*, 2002, Martin E. P. Seligman, PhD. In his book, Dr. Seligman discusses the pleasant life, the good life, and the meaningful life. Eventually, Dr. Seligman states that happiness is an emotion, but well-being is a construct. He began his studies by looking at happiness and then went deeper to create the Well-Being Theory, but his book, *Authentic Happiness*, sets the stage for meaning and purpose in one's life. Visit his website www.authentichappiness.org for some great tools and self-assessments.

From the world of business and leadership, we suggest the following:

- *Make It Matter: How Managers Can Motivate by Creating Meaning*, 2015, by Scott Mautz
- *The Why of Work*, 2010, by Dave and Wendy Ulrich
- *Good Business: Leadership, Flow, and the Making of Meaning*, 2003, by Mihaly Csikszentmihalyi

By no means is this an exhaustive list of books on the topic, but if you are interested in deepening your understanding of how meaning functions within in our lives, and how it can enhance your work as a leader, then the above selections are a great place to start. You can also review numerous other book titles in our bibliography.

The same is true for the following titles. While they support a deeper understanding of the impact of the leadership elements presented, they do not represent more than a surface scratch on the body of work that exists on the topics.

Engagement:

- *The Speed of Trust: The One Thing That Changes Everything*, 2006, by Stephen Covey and Rebecca R. Merrill
- *Lead from the Heart: Transformational Leadership for the 21st Century*, 2011, by Mark C. Crowley
- *Start with Why: How Great Leaders Inspire Everyone to Take Action*, 2009, by Simon Sinek

Empowerment:

- *A Leader's Legacy*, 2006, by James M. Kouzes and Barry Z. Posner
- *How the Way We Talk Can Change the Way We Work*, 2002, by Robert Kegan and Lisa Laskow Lahey

- *The Leader's Guide to Storytelling: Mastering the Art and Discipline of the Business Narrative*, 2011, by Stephen Denning

Expertise:

- *Presence: Exploring Profound Change in People, Organizations, and Society*, 2006, by Peter Senge, C. Otto Scharmer, Joseph Jaworski, Betty Sue Flowers
- *Flourish: A Visionary Understanding of Happiness and Well-Being*, 2011, Martin E. P. Seligman, PhD
- *Humility Is the New Smart: Rethinking Human Excellence in the Smart Machine Age*, 2017, by Edward D. Hess and Katherine Ludwig

These books are excellent sources of information on the elements of leadership presented in this book. We suggest several leadership blogs as well. Turning listening time during a workout or a commute into learning time has never been easier. There are a plethora of excellent podcasts on the topic of leadership and peak performance. Listed below, you will see a few of our favorites. Ultimately, the podcasts you will listen to will be the ones that resonate with you in terms of voice, content, and style. Listening to our suggestions is not essential because of the vast number of choices, but making the commitment to increase your learning time is highly recommended.

Podcasts:

- The John Maxwell Leadership Podcast
- Jocko
- Boss Files with Poppy Harlow: Conversations About business, leadership, and innovation
- Lead from the Heart with Mark C. Crowley
- Lead to Win with Michael Hyatt
- Dean Bokhari's Meaningful Show

Chapter 14

Tools for Measuring Impact

As our ability to measure positive emotion, engagement, meaning, accomplishment, and positive relations improves, we can ask with rigor how many people in a nation, in a city, or in a corporation are flourishing?

—Martin E. P. Seligman, *Flourish*

THE PERSONAL INVENTORY

Personal inventories offer leaders a way to develop an immediate plan for leadership development. The *Meaning-Centered Leadership* personal inventory provides leaders the opportunity to take a closer look at their leadership impact through the lens of *Meaning-Centered Leadership*. In a brief reflective session, you are able to self-assess your leadership on the elements of leadership presented in this book.

The self-assessment will help guide you through the next steps in leadership development. It is best practice to set aside at least an hour to provide yourself time to review the reflection questions associated with each element prior to responding to the survey questions. A deep and careful analysis of your current leadership practices will result in the best possible data being extracted.

The data from the personal inventory will help guide your next steps in developing the essential skills required of a *Meaning-Centered Leader*. By identifying your strengths and opportunities, you can develop a leadership improvement plan. Identify your lowest scores to understand what can be developed further, and identify your strongest scores to understand how to capitalize on your strengths.

Each of the elements of leadership presented in this book is represented by a group of five questions. As you answer these questions, it is important to reflect on your past and current leadership performance when ranking your scores. For example, the leadership element of trust is represented by the following five questions.

Personal Inventory
I have positive working relationships.
① ② ③ ④ ⑤
Strongly Disagree Disagree Disagree Neither Agree nor Disagree Agree Strongly Agree
My words are aligned with my actions.
① ② ③ ④ ⑤
Strongly Disagree Disagree Disagree Neither Agree nor Disagree Agree Strongly Agree
I trust my team members will do a good job.
① ② ③ ④ ⑤
Strongly Disagree Disagree Disagree Neither Agree nor Disagree Agree Strongly Agree
I lead with integrity and in an ethical manner.
① ② ③ ④ ⑤
Strongly Disagree Disagree Disagree Neither Agree nor Disagree Agree Strongly Agree
I promote a high level of trust among my team members.
① ② ③ ④ ⑤
Strongly Disagree Disagree Disagree Neither Agree nor Disagree Agree Strongly Agree

The personal inventory offers you a ranking scale matched with numerical values. Your score for each leadership element within each section conveys your score in that element: (1) Strongly Disagree, (2) Disagree, (3) Neither Agree nor Disagree, (4) Agree, (5) Strongly Agree. Take your time to gain accurate scores. For example, if you were assessing your score for question #1, your reflections would have to include examples of those positive relationships to rank yourself a 4 or a 5. The midrange score of 3 should be a default if neither positive nor negative examples drive your score in either direction. If you feel trusting your team members does not produce a

"Strongly Agree" or "Agree" score, your score would be below the midrange at either "Disagree" or "Strongly Disagree."

Using the chapter reflection questions and rereading sections as you progress through the inventory will help to sharpen your focus. It is important to read and process examples of both good and bad leadership. If you use strong emotional intelligence skills and are honest and mindful of your own levels of each question, you will be in a better position to improve upon your leadership skills.

You will find a complete personal inventory on all three elements of *Meaning-Centered Leadership* in the appendix. You will have a total score for each leadership element within the overall section. Your score for engagement will be a total of your scores in the three elements of engagement: trust, care and concern, and open communication with active listening. Each leadership element and the inventory questions are arranged as in the sample for trust. The same holds true for the elements of empowerment and expertise.

After completing each section, you will record the numerical values for each element and the totals within each section. This score sheet will allow you to see an overview of your current leadership practices as they relate to building meaning in your organization. Identifying your lowest areas will allow you to create a leadership improvement plan, as outlined below.

CREATING YOUR LEADERSHIP IMPROVEMENT PLAN

When reviewing your personal inventory, you can assess your strengths and areas for improvement to create your own personal leadership plan. For example, if your score report yields a low score in care and concern in the engagement skill set, you would return to that section of the book and focus on the reflection questions and review the strategies for success. By writing out answers to the reflection questions, you will gain insight that will point you in the direction of improving that area of your leadership. The personal inventory will allow you to be guided by your own self-reflections and direct you on what to focus on for improvement. You may wish to set a SMART goal in each of the three sections. If your scores indicate low scores in multiple sections, simply write multiple goals. However, all of your goals should follow the SMART[1] format.

It is critical that you set SMART goals associated with improving the leadership elements identified by the personal inventory. Some examples of SMART goals are given below.

SMART Goals Defined	
Specific	Clearly target an area you would like to improve upon. State the objective of your goal.
Measurable	Describe how your goal will be measured and how you hope to improve the measurable.
Achievable	Describe a specific action that will take place to help you achieve the desired goal.
Realistic	What can you reasonably expect to complete to reach your goal—provide concrete answers.
Time-Based	Apply a specific frame of time for implementation and reaching of the goal.

A sample SMART goal will follow the format presented here. From a personal inventory that identified recognition as a skill area for improvement, the following SMART goal was developed.

Sample SMART Goal	
Specific	In order to increase my score in recognition as measured by the M-CL personal inventory, I will increase the level of recognition I offer my staff.
Measurable	I will increase my score by one point, as measured by the M-CL personal inventory during the next six months.
Achievable	I will write three Wow cards per week and share weekly emails celebrating best practices I have observed.
Realistic	By increasing recognition during my walk-throughs, I will further engage and empower my teams.
Time-Based	Reassess six months from implementation.

To support your SMART goals, we suggest a weekly self-reflection journal. In this journal, you will reflect on whether you were able to meet your weekly goal. If you were not, it is imperative that you plan course corrections that allow you to stay on track with improving your *Meaning-Centered Leadership* skills. For example, did your walk-throughs get preempted by other job-related pressures? If that were the case, calendaring and protecting this time would be a sensible course correction. Did you lose sight of the importance of your goal? If that were the case, you might have to revisit the chapters on empowerment to help focus your energies to the changes required to fully deliver on your commitment to bring meaning to your organization.

THE WEEKLY REFLECTION JOURNAL

By three methods we may learn wisdom: First, by reflection, which is noblest;

Second, by imitation, which is easiest;
and third by experience, which is the bitterest.

—Confucius, Chinese teacher and philosopher

Weekly leadership reflection journals are a great goal. Reflection journals provide a solid learning opportunity for individuals. It is through reflection that we can understand our areas that need improvement. Also, by reflecting on your practices and writing them down, you can retain what worked well and what did not work well. By writing in your journal, you can solidify successes so they can be repeated and you can look for areas of improvement or areas that you can have fun changing and challenging next time.

Focused reflections on your goals will double the potential for them to inform and enhance your leadership. The key is allowing yourself the space for course corrections without scrapping your goal the first time it becomes difficult. Human behavior is often difficult to change, and you can expect it to be no different when attempting to change your own behavior.

As you begin your reflective journal practice, it is important to remember that research has found reflective practices in the workplace have led to increased productivity. You can replicate best practices more easily, and you can skip what did not work in the past. You do not have to repeat failures if they are noted for reference at a future date. Similarly, universities have discovered that the practice of self-reflection helps students use their resources more effectively. Self-reflective students also tend to outperform their non-reflective peers.

As leaders, we are in constant motion, so pausing for reflective journaling may feel like squandered time. Just remember that research supports reflective journaling as an effective way to increase performance. We suggest starting with as small a block of time as necessary for you to get started. If you are only able to reflect and write for ten minutes, start there. However, a thirty-minute block would be more ideal for taking the time to thoroughly review your practices from the previous week.

In addition to your SMART goals, reflecting on the elements of *Meaning-Centered Leadership* will provide ample opportunities for viewing your actions through the paradigm of implementation of these best practices. Create your goal, focus on accomplishing it, remeasure, and continue to grow. Lead, reflect, and improve. Those are the key processes for creating a pattern of lifetime growth and development. The *Meaning-Centered Leadership* framework provides you with ample areas for growing your leadership in an ongoing and cyclical nature. Personal and professional growth will enhance your impact and allow you to become a meaning-centered leader.

OBSERVATIONAL DATA

In chapter 5 we discussed the opportunities for developing engagement through MBWA. When you are present and attentive to the tasks that others are accomplishing, you have the opportunity to recognize and celebrate achievements. You also have the opportunity to gather observational data on how the work is being accomplished. An exemplary leader in the research described observing a manager treating an employee harshly. The leader used the opportunity to have a conversation with that manager. The outcome was that the manager received additional training to more effectively communicate expertise.

Your leadership should be informed by this type of data: that is, real-time actionable data that demonstrate whether the core operational values are being practiced. This type of data gathered by daily observations should be included in reflective practices for improvement. Sometimes, as in the above case, it may include the active practice of direct intervention to support the core values and to ensure adherence to the meaning-centered approach.

Generate an observational format that allows you to look for strengths and acknowledge excellence, while simultaneously measuring the enactment of the vision and core values. In the example from the research, the exemplary leader observed a manager violating a core value of fair treatment and dignity. The intervention addressed that and perhaps communicated to the leader that more work needs to be done to ensure the core values are enacted by all managers.

Using this type of data to inform practice will ensure the core values are more than just a slogan. In order to observe core values in action, they must be clearly articulated and communicated throughout the organization. Returning for a moment to the JetBlue example, one of their core values is fun. If that core value lives in the daily work of the JetBlue employees, it should be easy to find examples throughout the organization. From management to frontline staff, observational data should be collected as it relates to the core values.

Your observational data protocols need to be structured in a way that you are able to attend to and acknowledge core values in action. If the mission, vision, and core values are aligned and actionable, the leader should have a clear list of indicators to measure during observational data collection. That data collection should take place constantly, not just during structured observational rounds. Every interaction provides data points for a leader to examine evidence of the company culture in action.

THE LEADERSHIP SUPPORT TEAM

Whether you are leading a large organization or you are managing a small team, having a support team is essential. In healthy organizations, a support team may look like mentors and robust opportunities to interact with other organizational leaders. However, that is not always the case, and for entrepreneurs and small businesses, that leadership support team will have to be created. Whatever the case, focusing on the development of a leadership support team is essential. That may mean forging relationships with other leaders inside or outside of your organization, perhaps through associations, affiliates, or partner organizations. If you are not receiving coaching or mentoring, it is essential that you consider how to create those opportunities to ensure you have consistent and measured reflection and discussions about your leadership impact.

As we have stated in this book, continual development and growth is essential. Creating a support team is great practice for staying engaged and getting feedback from others. Hopefully, at this point, you are considering embarking on a mission to create meaning. Involving others in that journey is a great way to multiply your learning and learn from others. Consider creating a book club or leadership study group with the materials and resources offered within this text. Getting feedback and hearing from others will optimize your learning.

Working with a trusted leadership partner to engage in coaching sessions with each other is another way to create robust learning. The dialogue that takes place within these conversations may serve to enrich your leadership practices and increase your ROI from time spent in focusing on meaning-centered practices. The opportunity to coach others provides reciprocal learning on the topics being discussed. Others' viewpoints may spark ideas and help guide your thinking and deepen your development.

Another way to deepen your practice is to create a leadership retreat. Even if it is just for a few hours in an afternoon or morning, setting aside time for leadership development is an essential step to your future growth. Think of the impact of creating goals, sharing them with a leadership partner and then meeting to discuss those goals. This creates an opportunity for you to have an accountability partner that will ensure your leadership development is under constant growth. If your organizational structures don't support this type of robust focus on your leadership, it is essential that you take proactive steps to ensure your personal leadership development takes place. Your future, your organization, and the well-being of those you lead depend on your continual growth as a leader.

THE *MEANING-CENTERED LEADERSHIP* 360° ASSESSMENT

We cannot close this chapter without mentioning that several of the exemplary leaders in our research described using mentors and coaches to help them increase their leadership impact. We have designed our *Meaning-Centered Leadership* 360° Assessment (MCL-360°) as a tool to assist you in measuring your ability to build meaning in your organization. This multisource feedback tool is for those leaders who wish to maximize their effectiveness through feedback and coaching.

The MCL-360° Assessment requires a high degree of participation from others in your organization. It is also a best practice to invest in professional coaching as you develop and implement your leadership improvement plan. For that reason, the MCL-360° is available on our website. Easy-to-follow steps to download the survey for immediate use are available. You can also receive initial coaching sessions.

As Martin Seligman pointed out in his book *Flourish*, well-being is a construct that can be measured. The MCL-360° is designed to measure the key elements of *Meaning-Centered Leadership*. You will notice that many of the elements in Seligman's well-being construct are familiar and have been discussed in this book. By measuring your leadership skills on those elements, you will get specific feedback for reflection, improvement, and goal setting.

The MCL-360° Assessment is essentially a performance evaluation tool that collects and reports observations from colleagues. The MCL-360° Assessment offers several strengths when compared to other forms of feedback. Researchers have identified that they are superior to supervisory ratings. The inherent value of 360° feedback has been described as less likely to be deficient in criteria, while providing the participant with a valuable assessment of his or her behavior.

Researchers have described several strengths of gathering information via a 360° Assessment:

1. It allows for collection of data based on specific behavior.
2. It allows for analysis between rater groups and change over time.
3. It has the ability to sustain desired organizational change by groups and/ or individuals.

Additionally, the use of 360° Assessments has shown that they are an effective tool to help leaders initiate improvement in leadership acumen and interpersonal skills. In fact, leadership effectiveness has been shown to increase by as much as 60 percent in programs that use 360° Assessments in combination with coaching. The MCL-360° will allow leaders to sustain improvement on key elements of meaning that will allow for maximum personal and organizational growth.

Researchers express some disagreement on the content of a 360° Assessment. Some argue that the data should be reported as a numerical value with quantitative data only. However, qualitative data are said to provide deeper levels of information and details of an employee's thoughts, as opposed to strictly quantitative data. Our MCL-360° is designed to provide the participant with quantitative scores in engagement, empowerment, and expertise. Additionally, raters will have the opportunity to respond to open-ended questions. The qualitative feedback collected in the open-ended questions will provide additional data to guide and inspire change.

The feedback in a 360° can have significantly more value than self-initiated improvement. The MCL score you obtain when using the MCL-360° has been aligned to the goals of the *Meaning-Centered Leadership* framework. The feedback you receive will allow you to develop goals focused on that alignment. To be clear, the goal of the MCL-360° is to develop your skills in creating meaning in your organization. You will obtain data that are designed to allow you to create goals in all three areas of the *Meaning-Centered Leadership* framework.

We agree with researchers and practitioners who express that 360° feedback is relevant to help an organization develop a leader's potential. Through these assessments, leaders are able to better understand their personal strengths for driving performance, as well as their areas for potential growth. Through constant assessment and improvement, a leader is sure to drive a culture that creates meaning for themselves and others.

Chapter 15

Conclusion

Meaning-Centered Leadership
for Your Organization

> Your profession is not what brings home your weekly paycheck, your profession is what you're put here on earth to do, with such passion and such intensity that it becomes spiritual in calling.
>
> —Vincent Van Gogh

Meaning matters! As you have seen, research supports the imperative for meaning in the workplace in the twenty-first century and beyond. Without meaning, purpose, and significance, organizations will continue to struggle with employee engagement, which therefore affects the bottom line. As author Daniel Pink stated in his 2006 book, *A Whole New Mind: Why Right-Brainers Will Rule the Future*, "The future belongs to a very different kind of person with a very different kind of mind—creators and empathizers, pattern recognizers, and meaning makers."[1] Our book has offered numerous behaviors and strategies that demonstrate how to lead with meaning so your organization can become an exemplary organization.

Further, in his 2014 book, *The Work: My Search for a Life that Matters*, author Wes T. Moore stated that people want a job they love doing, a job they consider the "right job" and meaningful work. Doing what you love and loving what you do creates happiness. Doing the right job allows you to develop meaningful relationships with others, which in turn can lead to a rich and fulfilling life, both in and outside of work.

Laszlo Bock, head of people at Google and author of *Work Rules! Insights from Inside Google That Will Transform How You Live and Lead*, offers a list of ten steps to transform your organization. Give your work meaning is number one on his list! He states that a leader's job is to help others find meaning in their work. He points out that the work we do consumes a full half of our waking hours and a third of our lives. The growth of Google has, no doubt, been the product of very talented people working effectively toward a common goal, but according to Laszlo, the managers at Google put meaning at the top of their list. We hope that you too will put meaning at the top of your list and focus on creating a meaning-centered workplace.

The *Meaning-Centered Leadership* approach offers you the opportunity to answer the call of 181 CEOs from the Business Roundtable who recently signed a pledge to focus on creating dignity and meaning for each of their employees. This dramatic break from the past requires a new way of viewing and measuring leadership. The Business Roundtable group has established that the old bottom line of counting profit numbers is not enough. Leadership of the future must focus on a different set of metrics to determine their effectiveness. *Meaning-Centered Leadership* provides the paradigm for achieving the goal of focusing on dignity and meaning for workers while simultaneously pursuing goals for the organization.

In fact, this new vision of leadership and corporate governance requires an approach that breaks with the traditions of the past, a past that has been governed by placing the individual in a subservient role to the organization. A role that has harmed worker well-being and stymied the growth and productivity of organizations everywhere. *Meaning-Centered Leadership* provides the path to revisioning what it means for a leader to measure their success.

The new measure of leadership success must take into account the well-being of their workforce while simultaneously pursuing robust and profitable organizational outcomes. The measurement tools and strategies for growth provided in this book offer leaders a road map for that pursuit. It is a road map that must be used throughout your leadership journey. Reading the book once and considering data from the MCL-360° as an isolated event will not suffice. You must consider your journey toward becoming a meaning-centered leader as a grand adventure that you pursue throughout your career. We urge you to use the tools in this book in an ongoing attempt to be that rare leader who creates meaning for themselves, their organizations, and those whom they lead.

Leaders must consider the profound impact of becoming a meaning-centered leader. Creating a culture in which employees find meaning in their work is critical for the health and well-being of the individuals, as well as the organization. Remember, the quality of work effectively equals the quality of life. It is vital that, regardless of your industry, you implement the strategies that create meaning and purpose for your colleagues. We wish you much success on your journey to becoming a meaning-centered leader!

Appendix

Meaning-Centered Leadership
Engagement, Empowerment, Expertise

Personal Inventory

Score each of the following statements below based on how much you agree or disagree using the following scale.
Strongly Disagree=1, Disagree=2, Neither Agree nor Disagree=3, Agree=4, Strongly Agree=5

Engagement

Trust

I have positive working relationships	
My words are aligned with my actions	
I trust that team members will do a good job	
I lead with integrity and in an ethical manner	
I promote a high level of trust among team members	
TOTAL SCORE FOR TRUST	

Care & Concern

I care about the members of my team	
I convey concern for my team's well-being	
I show appreciation for individual and group contributions to the team's efforts	
I convey respect for all team members	
I value the work and talent of team member contributions	
TOTAL SCORE FOR CARE & CONCERN	

Active Listening with Open Communication

I feel there is open communication between management and staff	
I promote a safe environment for communicating ideas among team members	
I promote an open-door policy for team members to share their ideas	
Team input is taken into consideration when making decisions for the department	
Team members feel their opinions are valued	
TOTAL SCORE FOR ACTIVE LISTENING WITH OPEN COMMUNICATION	
ENGAGEMENT TOTAL	

Meaning-Centered Leadership
Engagement, Empowerment, Expertise

Personal Inventory

Score each of the following statements below based on how much you agree or disagree using the following scale.

Strongly Disagree=1, Disagree=2, Neither Agree nor Disagree=3, Agree=4, Strongly Agree=5

Empowerment

Collaborative Visioning

Team members show respect for one another	
I have a clear vision for my team	
I have a clear understanding of where the organization is headed and the plan to get there	
I include others in creating the vision for our organization	
I empower others to carry out the vision of our organization	
TOTAL SCORE FOR COLLABORATIVE VISIONING	

Recognition

I recognize good performers for their contributions to the team	
I recognize individuals for contributing ideas that result in process improvements	
I celebrate the team for the value they bring to the group effort	
I encourage celebration among team members for a job well done	
I celebrate team accomplishments with those inside and outside the organization	
TOTAL SCORE FOR RECOGNITION	

Enthusiasm

I convey a sense of excitement when I present new projects	
I provide support to keep the team energized and encouraged during times of change and/or challenge	
I convey enthusiasm and passion in my work	
I am an inspiration for my team	
I am committed to this organization	
TOTAL SCORE FOR ENTHUSIASM	
EMPOWERMENT TOTAL	

Meaning-Centered Leadership
Engagement, Empowerment, Expertise

Personal Inventory

Score each of the following statements below based on how much you agree or disagree using the following scale.

Strongly Disagree=1, Disagree=2, Neither Agree nor Disagree=3, Agree=4, Strongly Agree=5

EXPERTISE

Wisdom

I feel I am an effective leader	
I feel my decisions are based on data, research, and experience	
I have the knowledge and experience needed to successfully lead my team	
I lead by example by keeping control of my emotions and behaviors, even in high-pressure situations	
I support team members in their efforts to achieve their self-development goals	
TOTAL SCORE FOR WISDOM	

Optimism

I encourage a prioritization of innovation in the workplace	
I feel the decisions I make today will positively impact the future of this organization	
I have a clear understanding of the vision for the future of this organization	
I have a clear understanding of the steps needed to achieve the goals set for this organization	
I feel excitement when I envision the future of this organization	
TOTAL SCORE FOR OPTIMISM	

Humility

I regularly invite input from my team	
I acknowledge the input of others	
I have a growth mindset	
I am courageous in situations that require me to support my staff	
I am open to constructive feedback	
TOTAL SCORE FOR HUMILITY	

EXPERTISE TOTAL	

TOTAL M-C L SCORE: ENGAGEMENT + EMPOWERMENT + EXPERTISE	

Notes

PREFACE

1. Jim Clifton and Jim Harter, *It's the Manager* (New York, NY: Simon Schuster Publishers), 2019.

CHAPTER 1

1. Jim Clifton, *The State of the American Workplace* (The Gallup World Headquarters, Washington, DC, USA), 2018.
2. Clifton, *The State of the American Workplace*, 2.
3. Mark C. Crowley, *Lead from the Heart: Transformational Leadership for the 21st Century* (Bloomington, IN: Balboa Press, 2011), Podcast.
4. Robert Greenleaf, *Servant Leadership: A Journey into the Nature of Legitimate Power and Greatness* (Mahwah, NJ: Paulist Press, 2002), 58.
5. Viktor Frankl, *Man's Search for Meaning* (Boston, MA: Beacon Press, 1959), 105.
6. Mihaly Csikszentmihalyi, *Flow: The Psychology of Optimal Experience* (New York, NY: HarperCollins Publishers, 1990), 227.
7. Csikszentmihalyi, *Flow*, 3.

CHAPTER 2

1. Business Roundtable, "Business Roundtable Redefines the Purpose of a Corporation to Promote 'An Economy That Serves All Americans.'" Washington, DC, August 19, 2019. https://www.businessroundtable.org/business-roundtable-redefines-the-purpose-of-a-corporation-to-promote-an-economy-that-serves-all-americans.

2. Thomas Moore, *A Life at Work: The Joy of Discovering What You Were Born To Do* (New York, NY: Broadway Books, 2008), 159.

3. Gallup, *State of the American Workplace: Employee Engagement Insights for U.S. Business Leaders* (Washington, DC, 2013).

4. Csikszentmihalyi, *Flow*, 164.

5. Csikszentmihalyi, *Flow*, 154.

CHAPTER 4

1. Stephen R. Covey and Rebecca Merrill, *The Speed of Trust: The One Thing That Changes Everything* (New York, NY: Free Press, 2006), 2.

CHAPTER 6

1. Jim Collins and Jerry Porras, *Built to Last: Successful Habits of Visionary Companies* (New York, NY: HarperCollins, 2002), 208.

2. Scott Mautz, *Make It Matter: How Managers Can Motivate by Creating Meaning* (New York, NY: American Management Association, 2015), 28.

3. Robert Kegan and Lisa Laskow Lahey, *How the Way We Talk Can Change the Way We Work* (San Francisco, CA: A Wiley Imprint, 2001), loc. 7429.

4. Kerry Patterson, Joseph Grenny, Ron McMillan, and Al Switzler, *Crucial Conversations: Tools for Talking When Stakes Are High* (New York, NY: McGraw-Hill, 2012), 162.

5. James Kouzes and Barry Posner, *A Leader's Legacy* (Hoboken, NJ: Jossey-Bass, 2006), 36.

6. Kouzes and Posner, *A Leader's Legacy*, 47.

CHAPTER 7

1. Linda Ackerman-Anderson and Dean Anderson, *The Change Leader's Roadmap: How to Navigate Your Organization's Transformation* (San Francisco, CA: Pfeifer, 2010), 171.

2. Kouzes and Posner, *A Leader's Legacy*, 18.

3. Ackerman-Anderson and Anderson, *The Change Leader's Roadmap*, 171.

CHAPTER 9

1. M. R. Loughead, "A Transformational Model of Visionary Leadership," Ed.D. diss., University of Pittsburgh, 2009. Retrieved from ProQuest Dissertations Theses Global database (3384877), 3.

2. Kouzes and Posner, *A Leader's Legacy*, 26.
3. Greenleaf, *Servant Leadership*, 158.

PART III

1. Jean Hagen, *The Next Era of Human/Machine Partnerships* (Palo Alto, CA: Institute for the Future), July 12, 2017. www.iftf.org, 14.
2. Frankl, *Man's Search for Meaning*, 105.

CHAPTER 10

1. Paul Baltes and Ursula Staudinger, "Wisdom: A Metaheuristic (Pragmatic) to Orchestrate Mind and Virtue Toward Excellence," *American Psychologist, 55*(36) (2000): 122–136.
2. Patrick Lencioni, *The Five Dysfunctions of a Team* (San Francisco, CA: Wiley Imprint, 2002), 220.

CHAPTER 11

1. T. Maruta, R. C. Colligan, M. Malinchoc, and K. P. Offord, "Optimists vs. Pessimists: Survival Rate Among Medical Patients over a 30-Year Period," *Mayo Clinic Proceedings*. Retrieved from ProQuest Dissertations (RN074116504).
2. Martin Seligman, *Flourish: A Visionary New Understanding of Happiness and Well-Being* (New York, NY: Free Press, 2011), 66.
3. Warren Bennis and Burt Nanus, *Leaders: Strategies for Taking Charge* (New York, NY: HarperCollins, 2003), 58.
4. Seligman, *Flourish*, 27.

CHAPTER 12

1. Kouzes and Posner, *A Leader's Legacy*, 11.
2. Edward Hess and Katherine Ludwig, *Humility Is the New Smart: Rethinking Human Excellence in the Smart Machine Age* (Oakland, CA: Berrett-Koehler Publishers, Inc., 2017), 201–203.
3. J. Dame and J. Gedmin, "Six Principles for Developing Humility as a Leader," Harvard Business Review (2013): September 09, 2013. Retrieved from https://hbr.org/2013/09/six-principles-for-developing.
4. Robert Greenleaf, *Servant Leadership: A Journey into the Nature of Legitimate Power and Greatness* (Mahwah, NJ: Paulist Press, 2002), foreward.

5.   David Bobb, *Humility: An Unlikely Biography of America's Greatest Virtue* (Nashville, TN: Nelson Books, 2012).

6.   Ibid., 188.

CHAPTER 13

1.   Stephanie Vozza, Personal Mission Statements Of 5 Famous CEOs (And Why You Should Write One Too), FastCompany, February 25, 2014, Retrieved from https://www.fastcompany.com/3026791/personal-mission-statements-of-5-famous-ceos-and-why-you-should-write-one-too#:~:text=%E2%80%9CTo%20serve%20as%20a%20leader,and%20what%20you%20stand%20for.

2.   Ibid.

3.   Ibid.

4.   Business Roundtable, Press Release.

CHAPTER 14

1.   George Doran, "There's a SMART Way to Write Management Goals," *Management Review, 70* (1981): 35–36.

CHAPTER 15

1.   Daniel Pink, *A Whole New Mind: Why Right-Brainers Will Rule the Future,* Introduction (New York, NY: Penguin Group Inc.), 2006.

Bibliography

Ackerman-Anderson, Linda and Dean Anderson. *The Change Leader's Roadmap: How to Navigate Your Organization's Transformation.* San Francisco, CA: Pfeifer, 2010.

Axtell, Paul. *Make Meanings Matter: How to Turn Meetings from Status Updates to Remarkable Conversations.* Naperville, IL: Simple Truths, 2015.

Baltes, Paul and Ursula Staudinger. "Wisdom: A metaheuristic (pragmatic) to orchestrate mind and virtue toward excellence." *American Psychologist, 55*(36), (2000): 122–136.

Bandura, Albert. *Self-Efficacy: The Exercise of Control.* New York, NY: Worth Publishers, 1997.

Bartels, Barbara E. "Meaning makers: A mixed-methods case study of exemplary university presidents and the behaviors they use to create personal and organizational meaning." Ed.D. diss., Brandman University 2017. Digital Commons (10260006).

Bass, Bernard and Ruth Bass. *The Bass Handbook of Leadership: Theory, Research & Managerial Applications 4th Edition.* New York, NY: Free Press, 2008.

Bennis, Warren and Burt Nanus. *Leaders: Strategies for Taking Charge.* New York, NY: HarperCollins, 2003.

Blanchard, Kenneth & Spencer Johnson. *The One Minute Manager.* New York, NY: William Morrow and Company, 1981.

Bobb, David. *Humility: An Unlikely Biography of America's Greatest Virtue.* Nashville, TN: Nelson Books, 2012.

Bock, Laszlo. *Work Rules! Insights from Inside Google That Will Transform How You Live and Lead.* New York, NY: Twelve Hachette Book Group, 2015.

Boud, David, Rosemary Keogh, and David Walker. *Reflection: Turning Experience into Learning.* New York, NY: Routledge, 1985.

Business Roundtable. "Business Roundtable Redefines the Purpose of a Corporation to Promote "An Economy That Serves All Americans'." Washington, DC: August 19, 2019. https://www.businessroundtable.org/business-roundtable-redefines-the-purpose-of-a-corporation-to-promote-an-economy-that-serves-all-americans

Chalofsky, Neal. *Meaningful Workplaces: Reframing How and Where We Work.* San Francisco, CA: Jossey-Bass, 2010.

Clifto, Jim. *The State of the American Workplace.* Washington, DC, USA: Gallup, 2018.

Clifton, Jim and Jim Harter. *It's the Manager.* New York, NY: Simon & Schuster Publishers, 2019.

Collins, Jim. *Good to Great: Why Some Companies Make the Leap and Others Don't.* New York, NY: HarperCollins, 2001.

Collins, Jim and Jerry Porras. *Built to Last: Successful Habits of Visionary Companies.* New York, NY: HarperCollins, 2002.

Covey, Stephen R. *The 7 Habits of Highly Effective People: Powerful Lessons in Personal Change.* New York, NY: Free Press, 2004.

Covey, Stephen R. and Rebecca Merrill. *The Speed of Trust: The One Thing That Changes Everything.* New York, NY: Free Press, 2006.

Crowley, Mark C. *Lead From the Heart: Transformational Leadership for the 21st Century.* Bloomington, IN: Balboa Press, 2011.

Crowley, Mark C. and Tom Peters. "Tom Peters: A Leadership Legend in Rare Form." *Mark C. Crowley.* April 14, 2018. Podcast, Lead from the Heart.

Crowley, Mark C. and Stephen Covey. "Leadership & the Speed of Trust." *Mark C. Crowley.* August 30, 2019. Podcast, Lead from the Heart.

Csikszentmihalyi, Mihaly. *Flow: The Psychology of Optimal Exerience.* New York, NY: HarperCollins Publishers, 1990.

Dame, J. and J. Gedmin. "Six Principles for Developing Humility as a Leader." *Finweek.* (2013): 42–43.

Denning, Stephen. *The Leader's Guide to Storytelling: Mastering the Art and Discipline of Business Narrative.* San Francisco, CA: John Wiley & Sons, Inc., 2011.

Doran, George. "There's a S.M.A.R.T. way to write management's goals and objectives." *Management Review, 70,* (1981), 35–36.

Drucker, Peter. *The Practice of Management.* New York, NY: Harper Business, 1954.

Frankl, Viktor. *Man's Search for Meaning.* Boston, MA: Beacon Press, 1959.

Gallup, Inc. *The State of the American Workplace: Employee Engagement Insights for U.S. Business Leaders.* Washington, DC, 2013.

Greenleaf, Robert. *Servant Leadership: A Journey into the Nature of Legitimate Power and Greatness.* Mahwah, NJ: Paulist Press, 2002.

Hagen, Jean. *The Next Era of Human/Machine Partnerships.* Institute for the Future. Palo Alto, CA. July 12, 2017. www.iftf.org.

Hammond, Sue Annis. *The Thin Book of Appreciative Inquiry.* Bend, OR: Thinbook, 1996.

Hess, Edward and Katherine Ludwig. *Humility Is the New Smart: Rethinking human Excellence in the Smart Machine Age.* Oakland, CA: Berrett-Koehler Publishers, Inc., 2017.

Jackson, C. Edward. "Meaning-Centered Leadership: How exemplary technology leaders create organizational meaning." Ed.D. diss., Brandman University 2017. Digital Commons.

Karlgaard, Richard. "Innovation Rules." *Forbes.*

Kegan, Robert and Lisa Laskow Lahey. *How the Way We Talk Can Change the Way We Work.* San Francisco, CA: A Wiley Imprint, 2001.

Kofman, Fred. *The Meaning Revolution: The Power of Transcendent Leadership.* New York, NY: Crown Publishing Group, 2018.

Kouzes, James and Barry Posner. *A Leader's Legacy.* Hoboken, NJ: Jossey-Bass, 2006.

Kouzes, James and Barry Posner. *The Leadership Challenge: How to Make Extraordinary Things Happen in Organizations.* San Francisco, CA: Jossey-Bass, 2007.

Kouzes, James and Barry Posner. "To lead, create a shared vision." *Harvard Business Review, 87*(1), (2009): 20–21.

Leider, Richard J. *The Power of Purpose: Find Meaning, Live Longer, Better.* Oakland, CA: Berrett-Koehler Publishers, 2015.

Lencioni, Patrick. *The Five Dysfunctions of a Team.* San Francisco, CA: Wiley Imprint, 2002.

Loughead, M. R. "A transformational model of visionary leadership." Ed.D. diss., University of Pittsburgh, 2009. Retrieved from ProQuest Dissertations & Theses Global database (3384877).

Mautz, Scott. *Make It Matter: How Managers can Motivate by Creating Meaning.* New York, NY: American Management Association, 2015.

Maruta, T., R.C. Colligan, M. Malinchoc, and K. P. Offord. (2000). "Optimists vs. Pessimists: Survival Rate Among Medical Patients Over a 30-Year Period." *Mayo Clinic Proceedings.* Retrieved from ProQuest Dissertations. (RN074116504).

McFeely, Shane and Ben Wigert. "This Fixable Problem Costs U.S. Businesses $1 Trillion." *Gallup Workplace.* March 13, 2019. https://www.gallup.com/workplace /247391/fixable-problem-costs-businesses-trillion.aspx

McKee, Annie, Richard Boyatzis, and Frances Johnston. *Becoming a Resonant Leader: Develop Your Emotional Intelligence, Renew Your Relationships, and Sustain Your Effectiveness.* Boston, MA: Harvard Business Press, 2008.

Moore, Thomas. *A Life at Work: The Joy of Discovering What You Were Born to Do.* New York, NY: Broadway Books, 2008.

Moore, Wes. *The Work: My Search for a Life That Matters.* New York, NY: Spiegel & Grau, 2014.

Nanus, Burt. *Visionary Leadership: Creating a Compelling Sense of Direction for Your Organization.* San Francisco, CA: Jossey-Bass, 1992.

Ou, Amy, David Waldman, and Suzanne Peterson. "Do Humble CEOs Matter? An Examination of CEO Humility and Firm Outcomes." *Journal of Management, 44*(3), (2015): 1147–1173. https://doi-org.libproxy.chapman.edu/10.1177/01492 06315604187

Patterson, Kerry. *Influencer: The Power to Change Anything.* New York, NY: McGraw-Hill, 2008.

Patterson, Kerry, Joseph Grenny, Ron McMillan, and Al Switzler. *Crucial Conversations: Tools for Talking When Stakes are High.* New York, NY: McGraw-Hill, 2012.

Peters, Tom and Robert Waterman. *In Search of Excellence: Lessons from America's Best-Run Companies.* New York, NY: HarperCollins Publishers, 1982.

Pink, Daniel. *A Whole New Mind: Why Right-brainers Will Rule the Future.* New York, NY: Penguin Group Inc., 2006.

Rath, Tom. *StrengthsFinder 2.0.* New York, NY: Gallup Press, 2007.

Seligman, Martin. *Authentic Happiness: Using the New Positive Psychology to Realize Your Potential for Lasting Fulfillment.* New York, NY: The Free Press, 2002.

Seligman, Martin. *Flourish: A Visionary New Understanding of Happiness and Well-being.* New York, NY: Free Press, 2011.

Seligman, Martin. "The New Era of Positive Psychology." TED2004 Conference. Filmed February 2004. https://www.ted.com/talks/martin_seligman_the_new_era_of_positive_psychology?language=en

Senge, Peter. *The Fifth Discipline: The Art and Practice of the Learning Organization.* New York, NY: Doubleday, 2006.

Sinek, Simon. *Start With Why: How Great Leaders Inspire Everyone to Take Action.* New York, NY: Penguin Books, 2009.

Smith, Emily Esfahani. *The Power of Meaning: Finding Fulfillment in a World Obsessed with Happiness.* New York, NY: Broadway Books, 2017.

Ulrich, Dave and Wendy Ulrich. *The Why of Work: How Great Leaders Build Abundant Organizations That Win.* New York, NY: McGraw Hill, 2010.

Varney, John. "Leadership as Meaning Making." *Human Resource Management International, 17*(5), (2009), 3–5.

About the Authors

Dr. **Barbara E. Bartels** is a lifelong learner and educator. Dr. Bartels received her bachelor's degree from Illinois State University in Special Education, her master's in Business Administration (MBA) from St. Mary's College of California, and her doctorate of education in Organizational Leadership (EdD) from Brandman University, part of the Chapman University System. Her areas of study and research include education, business, entrepreneurship, and organizational leadership.

Her professional career has included extensive entrepreneurial work in both the education and business arenas. She has a passion for organizational leadership, change management, inspirational speaking, and motivational theory in the workplace. Her dissertation focused on *Meaning-Centered Leadership* and how exemplary leaders create meaning for themselves and others, thereby increasing productivity and employee engagement.

Dr. Bartels has presented nationally, including at the annual conferences of Association of California Community Colleges, Association of California School Administrators, and Noel Levitz. Dr. Bartels is also a university adjunct professor, focusing on business ethics and business leadership. She has been a dissertation committee member and coach and enjoys helping other students achieve meaning in their work and in their studies. Dr. Bartels recently presented a mock dissertation to over 200 doctoral students, faculty, staff, and guests.

When she is not pursuing her passion in speaking and coaching, she enjoys vacationing all over the world with her two children, Victoria and Ryan, spending time with close friends, and hiking through the Bay Area open spaces with her two dogs.

Dr. **C. Edward Jackson** is a lifelong educator with experience throughout the state of California and recently South Florida. He seeks to add value to others in all his endeavors. He is mission focused on living a meaningful life.

Dr. Jackson has helped lead public/private partnerships to national recognition and served as regional vice president for AdvancePath Academics. He has skill and experience in special education, blended learning, project-based learning, transformational change, and equity and access. Dr. Jackson also provides instruction and mentoring for future educators through his work as an adjunct professor at Brandman University.

When he is not pursuing his passion to improve society through education, he can be found on the water in South Florida, paddle boarding, boating, and swimming. He also enjoys doing yoga on the beach with his wife Gail, who is a South Florida Yoga instructor.

To book Dr. Bartels and Dr. Jackson for speaking opportunities, coaching, or mentoring, visit the website at www.meaningcenteredleadership.com or email at info@meaningcenteredleadership.com.

Meaning-Centered Leadership
Engagement, Empowerment, Expertise